SUPPLEMENTAL EXERCISES
FOR

THE EVERYDAY WRITER

Sixth Edition

Lex Runciman
LINFIELD COLLEGE

Carolyn Lengel

Kate Silverstein

Boston | New York

Copyright © 2016, 2013, 2009, 2005 by Bedford/St. Martin's.

All rights reserved. No part of this book may be reproduced, stored in a retrieval system, or transmitted in any form or by any means, electronic, mechanical, photocopying, recording, or otherwise, except as may be expressly permitted by the applicable copyright statutes or in writing by the Publisher.

Manufactured in the United States of America.

1 0 9 8 7 6
f e d c b a

For information, write: Bedford/St. Martin's, 75 Arlington Street, Boston, MA 02116   (617-399-4000)

ISBN: 978-1-319-02687-5

Preface

Supplemental Exercises for The Everyday Writer is a resource for teachers and students. Its exercises consist of sentences and paragraphs needing revision, most of them designed so that students can edit directly on the pages of this book.

The exercise sets are numbered to correspond to chapters in *The Everyday Writer* so that students can quickly locate help by following the cross-references in each exercise's instructions.

To help students check their own progress as they work, answers to the even-numbered exercise items appear in the back of this book. Exercises with many possible answers—those asking students to imitate a sentence or revise a paragraph, for example—are not answered here. Answers to the odd-numbered exercises are given in the instructor's answer key only, which is available for download at **macmillanhighered.com/everyday6e/catalog**.

If you have adopted *The Everyday Writer* as a text, you are welcome to photocopy any of these exercises to use for homework assignments, for classroom activities, or for quizzes. The book is also available for student purchase. Also available on our website are additional exercises for practice: **macmillanhighered.com/everyday6e**.

Contents

WRITING PROCESSES   1

1.1   The top twenty: A quick guide to troubleshooting your writing   1

CRITICAL THINKING AND ARGUMENT   5

10.1   Using the Toulmin system   5
10.2   Recognizing fallacies   5
11.1   Recognizing arguable statements   7
11.2   Demonstrating fairness   8

LANGUAGE   10

27.1   Identifying stereotypes   10
27.2   Identifying and revising sexist language   11
27.3   Rewriting to eliminate offensive references   12
28.1   Considering ethnic and regional varieties of English   13
29.1   Using appropriate formality   14
29.2   Determining levels of language   15
29.3   Checking for correct denotation   16
29.4   Revising sentences to change connotations   18
29.5   Considering connotation   18
29.6   Using specific and concrete words   20
29.7   Thinking about similes and metaphors   21
29.8   Recognizing correct spellings   22
29.9   Proofreading for spelling   23

29.10 Distinguishing among homonyms 24
29.11 Spelling plurals 25

STYLE 26

30.1 Combining sentences with coordination 26
30.2 Writing sentences with subordination 26
30.3 Using coordination and subordination 27
30.4 Emphasizing main ideas 28
31.1 Matching subjects and predicates 29
31.2 Making comparisons complete, consistent, and clear 30
31.3 Revising for consistency and completeness 31
32.1 Creating parallel words or phrases 32
32.2 Revising sentences for parallelism 33
32.3 Revising for parallelism and supplying necessary words 34
33.1 Revising for verb tense and mood 35
33.2 Eliminating shifts in voice and point of view 36
33.3 Eliminating shifts between direct and indirect discourse 37
33.4 Eliminating shifts in tone and word choice 38
34.1 Eliminating unnecessary words and phrases 39
34.2 Revising for conciseness 40
35.1 Varying sentence length and structure 41

SENTENCE GRAMMAR 42

36.1 Identifying verbs and verb phrases 42
36.2 Identifying nouns and articles 43
36.3 Identifying pronouns and antecedents 44
36.4 Identifying adjectives and adverbs 45
36.5 Adding adjectives and adverbs 45
36.6 Identifying prepositions 46
36.7 Identifying conjunctions 47
36.8 Identifying conjunctions and interjections 48
36.9 Identifying the parts of speech 49
37.1 Identifying subjects and predicates 50

37.2	Identifying subjects	51
37.3	Identifying predicates	52
37.4	Identifying prepositional phrases	53
37.5	Using prepositional phrases	53
37.6	Identifying verbal phrases	54
37.7	Identifying prepositional, verbal, absolute, and appositive phrases	55
37.8	Adding prepositional, verbal, absolute, and appositive phrases	56
37.9	Using verbal, absolute, and appositive phrases to combine sentences	57
37.10	Identifying dependent clauses	58
37.11	Adding dependent clauses	59
37.12	Distinguishing between phrases and clauses	60
37.13	Classifying sentences grammatically and functionally	61
37.14	Expressing subjects and objects explicitly	62
37.15	Using noun clauses, infinitives, and gerunds appropriately	63
37.16	Using adjective clauses appropriately	64
38.1	Using irregular verb forms	65
38.2	Editing verb forms	66
38.3	Distinguishing between *lie* and *lay*, *sit* and *set*, *rise* and *raise*	67
38.4	Deciding on verb tenses	67
38.5	Sequencing tenses	69
38.6	Converting the voice of a sentence	70
38.7	Using subjunctive mood	70
38.8	Writing conditional sentences	71
38.9	Using the present, the present perfect, and the past forms of verbs	72
38.10	Using specified forms of verbs	73
38.11	Identifying tenses and forms of verbs	75
38.12	Using verbs appropriately	75
39.1	Identifying count and noncount nouns	76
39.2	Using determiners appropriately; using articles conventionally	77
39.3	Using articles appropriately	78

40.1 Selecting verbs that agree with their subjects 79
40.2 Making subjects and verbs agree 80
41.1 Using subjective case pronouns 81
41.2 Using objective case pronouns 82
41.3 Using possessive case pronouns 83
41.4 Using *who, whoever, whom,* or *whomever* 84
41.5 Using pronouns in compound structures, appositives, elliptical clauses; choosing between *we* and *us* before a noun 85
41.6 Maintaining pronoun-antecedent agreement 86
41.7 Clarifying pronoun reference 87
41.8 Revising to clarify pronoun reference 88
42.1 Using adjectives and adverbs appropriately 89
42.2 Using comparative and superlative modifiers appropriately 90
42.3 Positioning modifiers 91
43.1 Revising sentences with misplaced modifiers 92
43.2 Revising squinting modifiers, disruptive modifiers, and split infinitives 93
43.3 Revising dangling modifiers 94
44.1 Using prepositions idiomatically 95
44.2 Recognizing and using two-word verbs 96
45.1 Revising comma splices and fused sentences 97
45.2 Revising comma splices 99
45.3 Revising comma splices and fused sentences 100
46.1 Eliminating sentence fragments 102
46.2 Revising a paragraph to eliminate sentence fragments 103
46.3 Understanding intentional fragments 104

PUNCTUATION AND MECHANICS 105

47.1 Using a comma to set off introductory elements 105
47.2 Using a comma in compound sentences 106
47.3 Recognizing restrictive and nonrestrictive elements 107
47.4 Using commas to set off items in a series 108
47.5 Using commas to set off parenthetical and transitional expressions, contrasting elements, interjections, direct address, and tag questions 109

47.6   Using commas with dates, addresses, titles, numbers, and quotations   110
47.7   Eliminating unnecessary commas   111
48.1   Using semicolons to link independent clauses   112
48.2   Revising misused semicolons   113
49.1   Using periods appropriately   114
49.2   Using question marks appropriately   115
49.3   Using exclamation points appropriately   116
50.1   Using apostrophes to signal possession   116
50.2   Using apostrophes to create contractions   117
51.1   Using quotation marks to signal direct quotations   118
51.2   Using quotation marks for titles and definitions   119
51.3   Using quotation marks appropriately   120
52.1   Using parentheses and brackets   121
52.2   Using dashes   123
52.3   Using colons   124
52.4   Using ellipses   125
52.5   Reviewing punctuation marks   126
53.1   Capitalizing   128
54.1   Using abbreviations   128
54.2   Spelling out numbers and using figures   130
55.1   Using italics   130
56.1   Using hyphens in compounds and with prefixes   132
56.2   Using hyphens appropriately   132

GLOSSARY OF USAGE   134

GU-1   Selecting the appropriate word   134
GU-2   Editing inappropriate words   135

ANSWERS TO THE EVEN-NUMBERED EXERCISES   137

Writing Processes

1.1 The top twenty: A quick guide to troubleshooting your writing

Revise each of the following numbered items to eliminate one of the twenty most common sentence-level errors written by first-year students. (See *The Everyday Writer*, Chapter 1.) Example:

College students are usually eager to spend ~~Spring~~ spring break having as much fun as possible.

1. After months of stressful schoolwork, students understandably want to spend the week relaxing or blowing off steam with there friends.

2. Popular spring break destinies over the years have included Mexican resorts, Florida beaches, and Caribbean islands.

3. A growing number of students, however, are beginning to recognize that its actually rewarding to spend vacation time in more useful ways.

4. According to one source, students may go on an alternative spring break to improve their résumé or to take an affordable trip, but they end up having an important emotional experience and building lifelong memories.

5. Moreover, as noted in a United Way blog entry, "What many students don't realize until they arrive is the impact it will have on their own lives". ("We Did Not Give Up")

6. According to Valeria Delgado, one student reluctantly volunteered at the Boys and Girls Club in Newark, New Jersey, over spring break in 2011 and finds that he enjoyed it much more than he thought he would ("Because Partying Is Too Mainstream").

Exercises 1.1 *The top twenty*

7. The Museum of Natural History is a favorite destination for New York City tourists. The dinosaur hall is probably the most popular exhibit, visitors find it fascinating to view these prehistoric creatures. The museum's Rose Center for Earth and Space is also not to be missed.

8. It is always delightful to walk through Central Park on a warm Summer day. Sunbathers set up towels on the lawn. People gather for concerts at the bandshell, while joggers move in groups along the reservoir. But the park is also magnificent during the stark, solitary days of winter.

9. When George Washington was inaugurated at Federal Hall on Wall Street in 1789 New York City was the capital of the United States, though this honor shifted to the District of Columbia the following year.

10. The city of New York is made up of five boroughs—the Bronx, Manhattan, Queens, Brooklyn, and Staten Island—and comprising an area of 322 square miles. It has more than 8 million residents, which makes New York the largest city in the United States.

11. People often make the trip to Brooklyn to visit Junior's Restaurant on Flatbush Avenue. Just to sample a slice of the famous cheesecake. Although the cake is available in a variety of flavors and toppings, the plain one is incredibly delicious!

12. The annual tree-lighting ceremony at Rockefeller Center unofficially marks the beginning of the holiday season in the Big Apple. Statues of silvery horn-blowing angels encircle the plaza leading to the tree and ice-skaters traverse the rink below. Taking center stage is the glorious tree itself, which twinkles with the glow of thousands of tiny lights. It is a magical time in the city for young and old alike.

13. The Statue of Liberty, the Empire State Building, and Times Square are among the most popular tourist destinations in New York. While these spots are certainly exciting, many find it more interesting simply amble through the city's varied neighborhoods. For those with an adventurous spirit, there are many delicious ethnic restaurants, charming shops, and uncrowded parks to discover.

14. The Harlem Renaissance took place during the thirties the upper Manhattan neighborhood became a focal point for African American artists, intellectuals, writers, and musicians. Some of the key figures of the period are Zora Neale Hurston, Langston Hughes, and Jean Toomer.

15. The New York City public transportation system which is known as the Metropolitan Transit Authority is a vast web of subways, buses, and ferries. For the uninitiated, it might appear too intimidating to navigate. However, it is certainly one of the quickest, cheapest, and most environmentally friendly ways to get around town!

16. Even John F. Kennedy was a fan of one local New York newspaper, because "I don't think the intelligence reports are all that hot. Some days I get more out of the *New York Times*."

17. For half a century, Ellis Island was the primary point of entry for immigrants arriving in the United States. Each of the new arrivals brought their own traditions, languages, and foods. Even today, New York City remains a vast melting pot of different cultures and ethnicities.

18. Many New Yorkers feel, that Times Square has become too commercialized in recent years. The old character of the area is lost as big chain stores and restaurants populate the streets. Others argue that change is inevitable and that the new places bring money and jobs into the area.

Exercises 1.1 — The top twenty

19. Each year the new student council members take-over the responsibilities of the former council.

20. The new law makes it illegal for drivers to talk on handheld cell phones, which many people are thrilled about. Unfortunately, it is obvious that many motorists are choosing to ignore this piece of legislation.

Critical Thinking and Argument

10.1 Using the Toulmin system

Use the seven-part Toulmin system to begin to develop an argument for one of the following questions. Here is the Toulmin system:

1. Make your claim.
2. Restate or qualify your claim.
3. Present good reasons to support your claim.
4. Explain the underlying assumptions that connect your claim and your reasons. If an underlying assumption is controversial, provide backing for it.
5. Provide additional grounds to support your claim.
6. Acknowledge and respond to possible counterarguments.
7. Draw a conclusion, stated as strongly as possible.

(See *The Everyday Writer*, section 10d.)

1. Should the Pledge of Allegiance include the phrase "Under God," or should that phrase be omitted?

2. Should schools be responsible for children's moral education, or should a child's moral development be solely the concern of the parents?

10.2 Recognizing fallacies

Locate any fallacies in the sentences below. Identify the name of the particular fallacy (for example, "bandwagon appeal"). Then write out a sentence or two explaining your reasoning. If a sentence contains an effective argument, write *no fallacy*. (See *The Everyday Writer*, section 10e.) Example:

> Instead of supporting the hunger initiative, that candidate believes that poor people should simply starve to death.

Exercises 10.2 — Recognizing fallacies

Fallacy: straw man

Explanation: This sentence makes the highly unlikely claim that a candidate who disagrees with the author's view must therefore want people to starve.

1. Addie almost made the dean's list last semester, and this semester she has been studying even harder and getting better grades. Chances are good that she will make the dean's list this time.

2. Successful, financially secure people have high credit scores. Find out how high your credit score is at getyourcreditreport.com.

3. A well-known Hollywood actress claims that this weight-loss plan is safe and effective, so I'm going to give it a try.

4. Everyone is talking about the new series on HBO. Don't miss the next episode this Sunday night!

5. Last summer's temperatures were much cooler than average. Global warming is clearly not a reality.

6. You obviously understand the importance of saving for retirement, and gold is the safest investment you can make.

7. It's completely unfair that I received a D on that English paper. After all, I've never gotten anything below a B before!

8. If we legalized the sale of marijuana, drug problems in this country would disappear.

9. It is true that we need real tax reform in this country, but I refuse to listen to the ideas of a senator who cheats on his wife and refers to grown women as "girls."

10. If the school budget doesn't pass, we can expect the exam results of the entire district to plummet.

11.1 Recognizing arguable statements

Indicate which of the following sentences are arguable statements of opinion and which are factual by filling in the blank after each sentence with *arguable* or *factual*. (See *The Everyday Writer,* section 11b.) Example:

The eradication of smallpox was the most important medical advance of the twentieth century. _arguable_

1. Every student should learn about the ravages of smallpox. _____
2. Smallpox killed at least a third of its victims throughout recorded history. _____
3. No disease could ever be more frightening than smallpox was to people five hundred years ago. _____
4. Smallpox decimated the native populations in the Americas during the era of European exploration and colonization. _____
5. Some scholars believe that the European explorers purposely infected native people with smallpox. _____
6. Columbus and other explorers must have realized that the people in the New World could have no immunity to European diseases. _____
7. The European interlopers and their virus destroyed cultures that were vastly superior to their own. _____
8. The World Health Organization declared in 1958 that eradicating smallpox was a worthy goal. _____

8 Exercises 11.2 *Demonstrating fairness*

9. Smallpox, the first disease to be wiped out by human efforts, was declared dead in 1980. _____

10. The samples of smallpox virus currently kept alive in maximum-security freezers should not be destroyed because terrorist groups might also store the virus. _____

11.2 Demonstrating fairness

Study carefully the following advertisement for the United Way. Then briefly answer each of the following questions.

Demonstrating fairness 11.2 Exercises

1. How do the writers of this advertisement establish common ground?
2. How do they demonstrate fairness?
3. How do they shape their appeal?

(See *The Everyday Writer*, section 11f.)

Language

27.1 Identifying stereotypes

Each of the following sentences stereotypes a person or a group of people. Underline the word or phrase that identifies the stereotyped person or group. In each case, be ready to explain why the stereotype may be offensive, demeaning, or unfair. (See *The Everyday Writer*, section 27a.) Example:

> **If you have trouble printing, ask a <u>computer geek</u> for help.**
>
> *Assumes that all computer-savvy people are geeky, which is not the case.*

1. For a blue-collar worker, he was extremely well-read.
2. All women just adore those flowery romance novels!
3. I wanted an Eastern European housekeeper because everyone knows they are the most thorough cleaners.
4. Did you see a chiropractor or a real doctor for your back problem?
5. Everyone in the South prefers the Confederate flag to that of the United States.
6. I know that he shouldn't have made those lewd remarks to the girl on the school bus, but boys will be boys.
7. How wonderful that you are adopting a child! Were you unable to have children of your own?
8. Those third graders were attentive, focused, and calm during the presentation. I guess they all took their Ritalin this morning.

27.2 Identifying and revising sexist language

The following excerpt is taken from a 1961 publication by the U.S. Department of Agriculture's Office of the General Counsel. Read it carefully, noting any language we might today consider sexist. Then try bringing the language up to date by revising the passage, substituting nonsexist language as necessary. (See *The Everyday Writer*, section 27b.)

Your Role as a Lawyer in the Department of Agriculture

A stimulating and rewarding career awaits you as a lawyer in the U.S. Department of Agriculture. You will be a member of a 200-man legal staff in the Office of the General Counsel, which performs all the legal work for the Department. You will find an opportunity to practice in the field of your interest. . . .

An attorney in the Office of the General Counsel has personal contact with the administrative officials who are his clients. He furnishes legal advice directly to these clients through all stages in the development, administration, and enforcement of departmental programs. The lawyer is not restricted to a narrow field of legal activity. He has an opportunity to engage in many legal functions that relate to his assigned program area. He gives oral advice, writes opinions and briefs, drafts all kinds of legal documents and regulations, drafts and interprets legislation, and engages in hearings and trial work.

Because of the volume and importance of the legal services that must be performed, an attorney in the Office of the General Counsel has an opportunity to handle complex and responsible legal work at an earlier stage in his career than in private practice. In addition, he is free from the personal and economic problems of individual clients.

27.3 Rewriting to eliminate offensive references

Review the following sentences for offensive references or terms. If a sentence seems acceptable as written, write C. If a sentence contains unacceptable terms, rewrite it. (See *The Everyday Writer*, Chapter 27.) Example:

> Passengers
> ~~Elderly passengers~~ on the cruise ship *Romance Afloat* will enjoy swimming, shuffleboard, and nightly movies.

1. The doctor and the male nurse had different manners when tending to the patients in their care.

2. All the children in the kindergarten class will ask their mothers to help make cookies for the bake sale.

3. The Oriental girl who works at the bank is always pleasant and efficient.

4. Acting as a spokesman and speaking with a southern twang, Cynthia McDowell, attractive mother of two, vowed that all elementary school teachers in the district would take their turns on the picket line until the school board agreed to resume negotiations.

5. If you get lost, just ask a policeman if he can assist you.

6. Seventy-six-year-old Jewish violinist Josh Mickle, last night's featured soloist, brought the crowd to its feet.

7. Our skylight was installed last week by a woman carpenter.

8. The interdenominational service was attended by Jews, Christians, Buddhists, and Arabs.

9. Blind psychology professor Dr. Charles Warnath gave the keynote address last night.

10. Catholic attorney Margaret Samuelson won her sixteenth case in a row last week.

28.1 Considering ethnic and regional varieties of English

Read the following examples by authors using ethnic and regional varieties of English. See if you can "translate" each of the passages into "standard" academic English. Once you have finished your translated sentences, write a brief paragraph (in "standard" academic English) discussing (1) the differences you detect between "standard" academic English and the ethnic or regional example, and (2) the effects that are achieved by using each variety of English. (See *The Everyday Writer*, sections 28b–c.)

"Hey!" squeaked Curtis, his expression amazed. "I got myself shot in the back!"

Beside him, Lyon lifted Curtis' tattered T-shirt, plain and faded black like the other boys' . . . gang colors. "Yeah? Well, you for sure be takin it cool, man. Let's check it out."

. . . Finally, he smiled and parted Curtis' arm. "It be only a cut. Like from a chunk of flyin brick or somethin. Nowhere near his heart. That be all what matter."
— JESS MOWRY, *Way Past Cool*

"Why don't you like me the way I am? I'm *not* a genius! I can't play the piano. And even if I could, I wouldn't go on TV if you paid me a million dollars!" I cried.

My mother slapped me. "Who ask you be genius?" she shouted. "Only ask you be your best. For you sake. You think I want you be genius? Hnnh! What for! Who ask you!"

— AMY TAN, *The Joy Luck Club*

29.1 Using appropriate formality

Revise each of the following sentences to use appropriate formality consistently, eliminating colloquial or slang terms. (See *The Everyday Writer*, section 29a.) Example:

> Although   be excited   as soon as
> I can ~~get all enthused~~ about writing, ~~but~~ I sit down to write, my
>   blank.
> mind goes ~~right to sleep.~~

1. At the conclusion of Jane Austen's classic novel *Pride and Prejudice*, the two eldest Bennett sisters both get hitched.

2. I agree with many of his environmental policies, but that proposal is totally nuts.

3. The celebrated Shakespearean actor gave the performance of a lifetime, despite the lame supporting cast.

4. We decided not to buy a bigger car that got lousy gas mileage and instead to keep our old Honda.

5. Often, instead of firing an incompetent teacher, school officials will transfer the person to another school in order to avoid the hassles involved in a dismissal.

6. After she had raced to the post office at ten minutes to five, she realized that she had completely spaced the fact that it was a federal holiday.

7. Desdemona's attitude is that of a wimp; she just lies down and dies, accepting her death as inevitable.

8. Moby Dick's humongous size was matched only by Ahab's obsessive desire to wipe him out.

9. The refugees had suffered great hardships, but now they were able to see the light at the end of the tunnel.

10. The class misbehaved so dreadfully in their regular teacher's absence that the substitute lost it.

29.2 Determining levels of language

For each of the scenarios below, note who the audience would be for the piece of writing. Then circle the level of formality that would be appropriate. Be prepared to explain your answer. (See *The Everyday Writer,* section 29a.) Example:

A Facebook group for people who are interested in Harley-Davidson motorcycles

Level of formality:

(informal)   formal

Audience: _____ others who share your passion _____

1. An email to a childhood friend across the country

   Level of formality:

   informal   formal

   Audience: _____

2. A letter requesting an interview in response to a help-wanted advertisement in the newspaper

   Level of formality:

   informal   formal

   Audience: _____

16   Exercises   29.3   *Checking for correct denotation*

3. A brochure explaining the recycling policies of your community to local residents

    Level of formality:

    informal   formal

    Audience: _____

4. A letter to the editor of the *Washington Post* explaining that a recent editorial failed to consider all the facts about health maintenance organizations (HMOs)

    Level of formality:

    informal   formal

    Audience: _____

5. A cover letter asking a professor to accept the late paper you are sending after the end of the semester

    Level of formality:

    informal   formal

    Audience: _____

29.3 Checking for correct denotation

Read each of the following sentences, looking for errors in denotation and using your dictionary as needed. Cross out every error that you find. Then examine each error to determine the word intended, and write in the correct word. If a sentence has no error, write C. (See *The Everyday Writer*, section 29b.) Example:

Peregrine falcons, once an endangered species, have ~~adopted~~ adapted to nesting in cities instead of wilderness areas.

29.3 Exercises

Checking for correct denotation

1. As recently as 1970, many people thought that the distinction of the peregrine falcon was inevitable.
2. The falcons' situation reached its apex that year, when there were no wild pairs of breeding peregrine falcons anywhere east of the Rocky Mountains.
3. Until 1965, the descent of the falcons was blamed on overdevelopment and hunting.
4. The real problem, which effected many other large birds, was the widespread use of the pesticide DDT.
5. By-products of the chemical remain for long periods in the body, and the falcons, which are at the top of the food chain, consumed concentrated doses.
6. DDT made the shells of the birds' eggs so brittle that they shattered when the falcons tried to incubate them.
7. The federal government banded the use of DDT, but the falcons needed even more assistance from humans.
8. Thin-shelled falcon eggs were taken from nests and replaced by plaster ones so the parent birds had the delusion that they were incubating eggs.
9. Meanwhile, the eggs were hatched in lavatories, and the chicks were returned to their parents' cliff-side nests and raised there.
10. Retrofitting the falcons to the East Coast has been wildly successful, and New York City, with its cliff-like skyscrapers, is now home to breeding pairs of peregrines.

29.4 Revising sentences to change connotations

The sentences that follow contain words with strongly judgmental connotative meanings. Underline these words; then revise each sentence to make it more neutral. (See *The Everyday Writer*, section 29b.) Example:

> The current NRA <u>scheme</u> appeals to patriotism as a <u>smokescreen to obscure the real issue</u> of gun control.
>
> The current NRA campaign appeals to patriotism rather than responding directly to gun-control proposals.

1. The Democrats are conspiring on a new education bill.
2. CEOs waltz away with millions in salary, stock options, and pensions, while the little people who keep the company running get peanuts.
3. America is turning into a nation of fatsos.
4. Tree huggers ranted about the Explorer's gas mileage outside the Ford dealership.
5. If the granola-loving mayor has his way, it will soon be a criminal offense to drink a twenty-ounce soda.
6. Naive voters often stumble to the polls and blithely yank whichever handles are closest to them.
7. Liberals constantly whine about protecting civil rights, but they don't care about protecting the flag that Americans have fought and died for.
8. A mob of protesters appeared, yelling and jabbing their signs in the air.

29.5 Considering connotation

Study the italicized words in each of the following passages, and decide what each word's connotations contribute to your understanding of the passage. Think of a synonym for each word, and see whether

Considering connotation **29.5 Exercises**

you think the new word would affect the passage. (See *The Everyday Writer*, section 29b.) Example:

> It is a story of extended horror. But it isn't only the horror that *numbs* response. Nor is it that the discoverer [Columbus] *deteriorates* so steadily after the discovery. It is the *banality* of the man. He was looking less for America or Asia than for gold; and the banality of expectation matches a continuing banality of *perception*.
> – V. S. NAIPAUL, "Columbus and Crusoe"

numbs: deadens, paralyzes
deteriorates: declines, gets worse
banality: ordinariness, triviality
perception: understanding, judgment

1. The Burmans were already *racing* past me across the mud. It was obvious that the elephant would never *rise* again, but he was not dead. He was breathing very rhythmically with long *rattling* gasps, his great *mound* of a side painfully rising and falling.
   – GEORGE ORWELL, "Shooting an Elephant"

2. Then one evening Miss Glory told me to serve the ladies on the porch. After I set the tray down and turned toward the kitchen, one of the women asked, "What's your name, *girl*?"
   – MAYA ANGELOU, *I Know Why the Caged Bird Sings*

3. We caught two bass, *hauling* them in *briskly* as though they were mackerel, pulling them over the side of the boat in a *businesslike* manner without any landing net, and stunning them with a *blow* on the back of the head.
   – E. B. WHITE, "Once More to the Lake"

4. The Kiowas are a summer people; they *abide* the cold and keep to themselves; but when the season *turns* and the land becomes warm and *vital*, they cannot *hold still*.
   – N. SCOTT MOMADAY, "The Way to Rainy Mountain"

5. If boxing is a sport, it is the most *tragic* of all sports because, more than any [other] human activity, it *consumes* the very excellence it *displays*: its very *drama* is this consumption.   — Joyce Carol Oates, "On Boxing"

29.6 Using specific and concrete words

Rewrite each of the following sentences to be more specific and more concrete. (See *The Everyday Writer,* section 29c.) Example:

The weather this summer has varied.

Going from clear, dry days, on which the breeze seems to scrub the sky, to the so-called dog days of oppressive humidity, July and August have offered two extremes of weather.

1. The child played on the beach.
2. She couldn't wait to leave her job.
3. The attendant came toward my car.
4. Children sometimes behave badly in public.
5. The entryway of the building was dirty.
6. They started the trip in Spain.
7. My neighbor is a nuisance.
8. Sunday dinner was good.
9. Meg loved gardening.
10. The rock concert made him feel young again.

29.7 Thinking about similes and metaphors

Identify the similes and metaphors in the following numbered items, and decide how each contributes to your understanding of the passage or sentence in which it appears. (See *The Everyday Writer*, section 29d.) Example:

> The tattoo he had gotten as a teenager, now a blue bruise underneath the word "Mom," remained his favorite souvenir.

a blue bruise (metaphor): makes vivid the tattoo's appearance

1. The fog hangs among the trees like veils of trailing lace.
   – STEPHANIE VAUGHN, "My Mother Breathing Light"

2. The clouds were great mounds of marshmallow fluff heaped just below the wings of the passing airplane.

3. The migraine acted as a circuit breaker, and the fuses have emerged intact. – JOAN DIDION, "In Bed"

4. As Serena began to cry, James felt as if someone had punched him in the stomach.

5. Black women are called, in the folklore that so aptly identifies one's status in society, "the mule of the world," because we have been handed the burdens that everyone else — everyone else — refused to carry.
   – ALICE WALKER, *In Search of Our Mothers' Gardens*

6. John's mother, Mom Willie, who wore her Southern background like a magnolia corsage, eternally fresh, was robust and in her sixties.
   – MAYA ANGELOU, "The Heart of a Woman"

7. According to Dr. Seuss, the Grinch is a bad banana with a greasy black peel.

8. I was watching everyone else and didn't see the waitress standing quietly by. Her voice was deep and soft like water moving in a cavern.
   – WILLIAM LEAST HEAT MOON, "In the Land of 'Coke-Cola'"

9. The clicking sounds of the rotary phone were as old-fashioned and charming as the song of a square-dance caller.

10. My horse, when he is in his stall or lounging about the pasture, has the same relationship to pain that I have when cuddling up with a good murder mystery—comfort and convenience have top priority.
    – VICKI HEARNE, "Horses in Partnership with Time"

29.8 Recognizing correct spellings

Underline the correct spelling from the pair of words in parentheses in each of the following sentences. (See *The Everyday Writer*, sections 29f–g.) Example:

Have you ever taken the food list (chalenge/<u>challenge</u>)?

1. You can (easily/easyly) find the list online of the 100 foods to eat before you (die/dye).

2. According to some Internet (cites/sites), most people have eaten only twenty or fewer of these items.

3. (Their/There) are some unusual items on the list, (includeing/including) crickets, frogs' legs, and kangaroo.

4. My (freinds/friends) and I took the quiz, and I was (surprised/surprized) to see the things they have eaten.

5. They (to/too) were shocked to learn what I had (tried/tryed): venison, squirrel, and rabbit stew, all while spending the summer at my boyfriend's hunting camp.

6. The "straight-to-video" strategy was once reserved only for (truely/truly) bad movies that were sure to (loose/lose) money in theaters.

7. But independent filmmakers have also (successfully/sucessfully) created unique straight-to-video hits for specialized audiences.

8. Straight-to-video films — (which/witch) today usually go straight to DVD — are often made by young filmmakers who have a hard time getting their films (accepted/excepted) in theaters.

9. Films that appear first in stores may or may not be (especially/specially) good, and they have usually cost very little money to make.

10. Spending (a lot/alot) of money on making a movie does not (neccessarily/necessarily) mean that the movie will be good, in any case.

29.9 Proofreading for spelling

Proofread the following paragraph, and correct any spelling errors that you find. (See *The Everyday Writer,* sections 29f–g.)

    The family was vary excited about there beech holiday. They had weighted years too come up with the money, scrimping an saving every penny they could. The children where particularly looking for ward to going on the aerplane. When they arrived at there motel, they discovered that they had ben somewhat miss led, for the front roome did not face the oceann. They decided too make the best off it. Immediately, they through on there bathing suites and headed for the see. The parents watched their little brood jumping an splashing in the waives and smiled at each other contentedley.

29.10 Distinguishing among homonyms

Choose the appropriate word in each set of parentheses. (See *The Everyday Writer*, section 29f.) Example:

Antifreeze can have a toxic (affect/<u>effect</u>) on pets.

People need antifreeze in (their/there/they're) cars in cold (weather/whether). Unfortunately, antifreeze also tastes (grate/great) to cats and dogs, who drink it from the greenish puddles commonly (scene/seen) on asphalt. Antifreeze made of ethylene glycol causes kidney failure and has (lead/led) to the deaths of many pets. (Its/It's) not (to/too/two) hard to protect (your/you're) animals from antifreeze poisoning, however. First, (buy/by) antifreeze that does not contain ethylene glycol, in spite of (its/it's) higher cost. Second, do not let pets wander out of (cite/sight/site) when they are outdoors. Third, if a pet acts sick, get help even if the animal (seams/seems) to improve — animals with antifreeze poisoning appear to feel better shortly before they (die/dye). And finally, give the animal vodka or other liquor as an antidote, but only if (their/there/they're) is no way for a veterinarian to look at your pet immediately.

29.11 Spelling plurals

Form the plural of each of the following words. (See *The Everyday Writer*, section 29g.) Example:

    fox   foxes

1. deer
2. curriculum
3. leech
4. wolf
5. cherry
6. man-of-war
7. echo
8. spy
9. analysis
10. box
11. wish
12. mother-in-law

Style

30.1 Combining sentences with coordination

Using the principles of coordination to signal equal importance or to create special emphasis, combine and revise the following ten short sentences into several longer and more effective ones. Add or delete words as necessary. (See *The Everyday Writer,* Chapter 30, especially section 30a.)

The beach was deserted. I wondered where all the surfers were. The waves were calling to me. The sand was burning my feet. I walked toward the ocean. I let the water splash my ankles. Standing at the water's edge, I watched for a very long time. I knew it was getting late. I had to make my way back. I picked up a few seashells to give to my little sister.

30.2 Writing sentences with subordination

Combine each of the following sets of sentences into one sentence that uses subordination to signal the relationships among ideas. Add or delete words as necessary. (See *The Everyday Writer,* section 30b.) Example:

> **The bus swerved to avoid hitting a dog.**
> **It narrowly missed a car.**
> **The car was in the bus driver's blind spot.**
>
> When the bus swerved to avoid hitting a dog, it narrowly missed a car that was in the bus driver's blind spot.

1. The newlyweds did not have a big budget.

   They wanted to go somewhere special for their honeymoon.

   They decided to go to the famous resort in the off-season.

2. They had planned to go to Paris in the spring.

   They were forced to change their plans.

   Their eldest child became ill.

3. Steve Jobs founded Apple Computer in 1976.

   He was fired in 1985 by the board of directors.

   They didn't agree with his management style.

4. It was a gray, rainy day.

   We enjoyed driving along the Pacific Coast Highway.

   It is very scenic.

   It became too overcast to see anything.

5. The cruise ship had three different restaurants to choose from.

   We picked the café near the ballroom.

   We wanted to dance until dawn.

30.3 Using coordination and subordination

Revise the following paragraph, using coordination and subordination where appropriate to clarify the relationships between ideas. (See *The Everyday Writer*, Chapter 30, especially sections 30a–b.)

Wasabi is a root. It originally came from Japan. Wasabi is prized as a spice. It can cost as much as $100 per pound. It is related to horseradish. Wasabi has the same sinus-clearing effect that horseradish has. It grows in icy mountain streams. Wasabi is difficult to grow on farms. American farmers are trying to perfect techniques for growing wasabi in this country. One Californian has invested in expensive technology for his wasabi farm. His name is Roy Carver. He is the largest producer of wasabi outside of Japan.

People have tried to sneak onto his farm to see how he grows wasabi. He now keeps the location of his wasabi farm a closely guarded secret.

30.4 Emphasizing main ideas

Revise each of the following sentences to highlight what you take to be the main or most important ideas. (See *The Everyday Writer*, section 30c.) Example:

Theories about dinosaurs run the gamut—simple lizards, fully adapted warmblooded creatures, hybrids of coldblooded capabilities.

1. A crowd gathered, the stranded whale wriggled off the sandy beach, and a chorus of seagulls cried shrilly.

2. The blogger known only as Atrios writes political commentary successfully enough to attract loyal readers, at least one lawsuit, and plenty of advertisers.

3. All medical papers, whether initial investigation, presentation of final statistics, or reports on work in progress, must undergo rigorous scrutiny.

4. Coast Guard personnel conduct boating safety classes, sometimes must risk their own lives to save others, and monitor emergency radio channels.

5. Ever since the iPhone became popular, apps have been created that allow us to play games, instantly recognize constellations in the night sky, and record voice memos.

6. Large numbers of people don't bother with recycling because it takes up time, uses up storage space, and can lead to unpleasant odors, even though many people agree that recycling is generally beneficial.

7. The word *marathon* comes from the ancient Greek legend that a runner delivered a victory message from the Battle of Marathon to Athens, which was twenty-six miles away, as many people have heard.

8. Although industrial dairy farmers insist that bovine growth hormone is harmless, the public wonders whether it could have strange effects on the human endocrine system, cause cancer, or lead to digestive trouble.

9. Ansel Adams was a photographer, his color photographs were published to critical acclaim after his death, and he was generally known for his stark, black-and-white landscape photographs.

10. This all-in-one plant food I bought led to the largest tomato crop I have ever seen, kept the bugs away, and prevented fungus from forming.

31.1 Matching subjects and predicates

Revise each of the following sentences in two ways to make sure its structure is consistent in grammar and meaning. (See *The Everyday Writer*, section 31b.) Example:

By studying African American folklore and biblical stories have influenced Toni Morrison's fiction.

African American folklore and biblical stories have influenced Toni Morrison's fiction.

Toni Morrison's study of African American folklore and biblical stories has influenced her fiction.

1. Toni Morrison's grandmother, who moved to Ohio from the South with only fifteen dollars to her name, and Morrison had great respect for her.

2. In her books, many of which deal with the aftermath of slavery, often feature strong women characters.

Exercises 31.2 Making comparisons complete, consistent, and clear

3. Published in 1970, Morrison's first novel, *The Bluest Eye*, the story of a young African American girl who wants to look like her Shirley Temple doll.

4. Although Morrison's depictions of African American families and neighborhoods are realistic, but they also include supernatural elements.

5. An important character in Morrison's 1977 novel *Song of Solomon* is about Pilate, a woman with magical powers.

6. *Song of Solomon*, hailed as a masterpiece, winning the National Book Critics Circle Award in 1978.

7. Morrison's fame as a writer won the Pulitzer Prize in fiction in 1988 for *Beloved*.

8. The title character in *Beloved* features the ghost of a murdered infant inhabiting the body of a young woman.

9. When reading *Beloved* makes the horrors of American slavery seem immediate and real.

10. In 1993, Toni Morrison, who became the first African American woman to be awarded the Nobel Prize in Literature.

31.2 Making comparisons complete, consistent, and clear

Revise each of the following sentences to eliminate any inappropriate elliptical constructions; to make comparisons complete, logically consistent, and clear; and to supply any other omitted words that are necessary for meaning. (See *The Everyday Writer*, section 31e.) Example:

> American soccer (known as football in most of the world) is more popular in Europe than ^it is in^ the United States.

Revising for consistency and completeness **31.3** **Exercises**

1. Records show that the average sea temperature in the past decade is higher.
2. As the counselor pointed out, some jobs require more education.
3. Travel on a commercial airplane is statistically safer than a car.
4. Heart disease kills more people than cancer.
5. Taking out loans to pay for college may seem financially risky, but forgoing a college education even riskier.
6. Is the U.S. national debt higher than other countries?
7. Andrew needs a ride to soccer practice, Susie needs one to her piano lesson, and Joe to the hockey rink.
8. Argentina and Peru were colonized by Spain, and Brazil by Portugal.
9. Are citizens of the United States now as safe or safer than they were before September 11, 2001?
10. I enjoyed the movie more than John.

31.3 Revising for consistency and completeness

Revise this passage so that all sentences are grammatically and logically consistent and complete. (See *The Everyday Writer*, Chapter 31.)

A concentrated animal feeding operation, or CAFO, is when a factory farm raises thousands of animals in a confined space. Vast amounts of factory-farm livestock waste, dumped into giant lagoons, which are an increasingly common sight in rural areas of this country. Are factory-farm operations healthy for their neighbors, for people in other parts of the country, and the environment? Many people think that these operations damage our air and water more than small family farms.

Exercises

32.1 Creating parallel words or phrases

One problem with factory farming is the toxic waste that has contaminated groundwater in the Midwest. In addition, air quality produces bad-smelling and sometimes dangerous gases that people living near a CAFO have to breathe. When a factory farm's neighbors complain may not be able to close the operation. The reason is because most factory farms have powerful corporate backers.

Not everyone is angry about the CAFO situation; consumers get a short-term benefit from a large supply of pork, beef, and chicken that is cheaper than family farms can raise. However, the more people know about factory farms, the less interest in supporting their farming practices.

32.1 Creating parallel words or phrases

Complete the following sentences, using parallel words or phrases in each case. (See *The Everyday Writer,* sections 32a–b.) Example:

The wise politician _promises the possible_, _effects the unavoidable_, and _accepts the inevitable_.

1. My favorite pastimes include _____, _____, and _____.

2. This summer, I want to _____, _____, and _____.

3. My motto is _____, _____, and _____.

4. In preparation for his wedding day, the groom _____, _____, and _____.

Revising sentences for parallelism **32.2** Exercises

5. _____, _____, and _____ are activities my grandparents enjoy.

6. When he got his promotion, he _____, _____, and _____.

7. You should _____, _____, or _____ before you invite six guests for dinner.

8. The college athlete realized she would need to both _____ and _____.

9. Graduates find that the job market _____, _____, and _____.

10. Just as _____, so has _____.

32.2 Revising sentences for parallelism

Revise the following sentences to eliminate any errors in parallel structure. (See *The Everyday Writer*, Chapter 32.) Example:

Pérez Prado's orchestra was famous for playing irresistible rhythms and ~~because it turned~~ the mambo into a new dance craze.
    ^turning

1. The latest dance steps and wearing festive party clothes were necessities for many teenagers in the 1950s.

2. Many people in this country remember how they danced to the mambo music of the 1950s and listening to that era's Latin bands.

3. Older dancers may recall Rosemary Clooney, Perry Como, and Ruth Brown singing mambo numbers and Pérez Prado's band had a huge hit, "Cherry Pink and Apple Blossom White."

Exercises 32.3 *Revising for parallelism and supplying words*

4. Growing up near Havana and a student of classical piano, Pérez Prado loved Cuban music.

5. Pérez Prado wanted not only to play Cuban music but also he wanted to combine it with elements of jazz.

6. Playing piano in Havana nightclubs, arranging music for a Latin big band, and the jam sessions he joined with the band's guitarists gave him the idea for a new kind of music.

7. The result was a new dance phenomenon: mambo music was born, and Pérez Prado, who became known as "King of the Mambo."

8. Prado conducted his orchestra with hand waving, head and shoulder movements, and by kicking his feet high in the air.

9. His recordings feature syncopated percussion, wailing trumpets, and Prado shouted rhythmically.

10. Pérez Prado, innovative and a great musician, died in 1989.

32.3 Revising for parallelism and supplying necessary words

Revise the following paragraph to maintain parallelism where it exists and to supply all words necessary for clarity, grammar, and idiom in parallel structures. (See *The Everyday Writer*, Chapter 32.)

Family gatherings for events like weddings, holidays, and going on vacation are supposed to be happy occasions, but for many people, getting together with family members causes tremendous stress. Everyone hopes to share warm memories and for a picture-perfect family event. Unfortunately, the reality may include an uncle who makes offensive remarks, a critical mother, or anger at a spouse who doesn't lift a finger to help. Neither difficult relatives nor when things go wrong will necessarily ruin a big family gathering, however. The trick is to plan for problems and being able to adapt. Family members who are not flexible, not pleasant to be around, or willing to do their part may always be a problem for their relatives. However, people who try to make a family gathering a success will almost always either be able to enjoy the event or laugh about it later.

33.1 Revising for verb tense and mood

Revise any of the following sentences in which you find unnecessary shifts in verb tense or in mood. If a sentence is correct as written, write C. (See *The Everyday Writer,* sections 33a–b.) Examples:

> The doctor examined six patients, but she ~~washes~~ ^washed^ her hands only four times.
>
> Scrub with soap for ten to fifteen seconds and ~~you should~~ rinse thoroughly.

1. More than 150 years ago, a Hungarian doctor discovered that doctors who deliver babies and did not thoroughly wash their hands often spread a deadly infection to new mothers.

2. Today, we know better. It is common knowledge that unclean hands transmit germs.

3. Most people learn as children that keeping their hands clean is very important. However, sometimes they forgot this lesson in later life.

4. All health care workers should know that they had to keep their hands clean.

5. Unfortunately, a new study indicates that a high percentage of busy health care workers did not wash their hands often enough.

6. Hand washing can be repetitive, time consuming, and boring, but it should be crucial to patient safety in every hospital.

7. Approximately 5 percent of the patients who were admitted to hospitals this year will get an infection there. Some of those infections may be deadly.

8. The bacteria that cause these infections could not travel through the air. They require physical contact to move from place to place.

9. If all hospital workers were to wash their hands regularly, fewer infections travel from patient to patient.

10. Wash your hands frequently, and you should follow these instructions even if your skin gets dry.

33.2 Eliminating shifts in voice and point of view

Revise each of the following sentences to eliminate an unnecessary shift in voice or point of view. (See *The Everyday Writer*, sections 33c–d.) Example:

The dancers performed on a low stage as a jig ~~was played by a fiddler~~. fiddler played a

1. I liked the sense of individualism, the crowd yelling for you, and the feeling that I was in command.

2. The police sent protesters to a distant "free speech zone," but supporters were allowed to stand along the motorcade route.

3. When someone says "roommate" to a high school senior bound for college, thoughts of no privacy and potential fights are conjured up.

4. Sea anemones thrive in coastal tide pools, but it cannot survive outside the water for very long.

5. Suddenly we heard an explosion of wings off to our right, and you could see a hundred or more ducks lifting off from the water.

6. If one has been pleased with a purchase on our site, would you consider reviewing it?

7. I had planned to walk home after the movie, but you shouldn't be on campus alone after dark.

8. Many home-improvement projects are completed by do-it-yourselfers, but some people prefer to hire contractors.

9. We knew that emails promising free gifts were usually scams, but you couldn't resist clicking on the link just to see.

10. The slow food movement emerged in France several decades ago; they set out to oppose the spread of fast-food chains in Europe.

33.3 Eliminating shifts between direct and indirect discourse

To eliminate the shifts between direct and indirect discourse in the following sentences, put the direct discourse into indirect form. (See *The Everyday Writer*, section 33e.) Example:

> Steven Pinker ~~stated~~ *states* that ~~my~~ *his* book is meant for people who use language and respect it.

1. Richard Rodriguez acknowledges that intimacy was not created by a language; "it is created by intimates."

2. She said that during a semester abroad, "I really missed all my friends."

Exercises 33.4 *Eliminating shifts in tone and word choice*

3. The bewildered neighbor asked him, "What the heck he thought he was doing on the roof?"

4. Loren Eiseley feels an urge to join the birds in their soundless flight, but in the end he knows that he cannot, and "I was, after all, only a man."

5. The instructor told us, "Please read the next two stories before the next class" and that she might give us a quiz on them.

33.4 Eliminating shifts in tone and word choice

Revise each of the following sentences to eliminate shifts in tone and word choice. (See *The Everyday Writer*, section 33f.) Example:

> You should try
> ~~It would behoove you to endeavor~~ to cut down on all those sweets.

1. I am astounded by the number of emails I receive each day trying to flog meds to me.

2. The Chinese invented noodles, even though lots of people think that the Italians must have come up with that bright idea.

3. Most commuters keep to a predictable schedule, hopping a bus or train to the 'burbs at the same time each night.

4. The Guggenheim exhibit of African works of art, often misunderstood and undervalued by Western art historians, is a heck of a show.

5. After she had yanked little William out of the busy street by the strap of his overalls, she tendered a verbal rebuke that left both the child and his mother sniffling.

34.1 Eliminating unnecessary words and phrases

Make each of the following sentences clear and concise by eliminating unnecessary words and phrases and by making additions or revisions as needed. (See *The Everyday Writer,* Chapter 34.) Example:

The ~~incredible, unbelievable~~ feats that Houdini performed amazed ~~and astounded~~ all his audiences ~~who came to see him~~.

1. Harry Houdini, whose real birth name was Ehrich Weiss, made the claim that he had been born in Appleton, Wisconsin, but in actual fact he was born into the world in Budapest, Hungary.

2. Shortly after Houdini's birth, his family moved to Appleton, where his father served as the one and only rabbi in Appleton at that point in time.

3. Houdini gained fame as a really great master escape artist.

4. His many numerous escapes included getting out of a giant sealed envelope without tearing it and walking out of jail cells that were said to be supposedly escape proof.

5. Before his untimely early death, Houdini told his brother to burn and destroy all papers describing how Houdini's illusions worked.

6. Clearly, it is quite obvious that Houdini did not want anyone at all to know his hidden secrets.

7. Part of the explanation for Houdini's escape artistry lies in the fact that his physique was in absolutely peak physical condition.

8. Houdini's tremendous control over almost every single individual muscle allowed him to contort his body into seemingly impossible positions.

9. After his mother's death, Houdini grew interested in spiritualism until he discovered that the mediums who were the people running the séances were frauds trying to do nothing more than bilk and cheat their customers.

10. On his deathbed, Houdini promised his wife that he would try and attempt to make contact with her from beyond the grave, but so far, he has never been able to get in touch yet.

34.2 Revising for conciseness

Revise the following paragraph so that each sentence is as concise as possible. Combine or divide sentences if necessary. (See *The Everyday Writer*, Chapter 34.)

At the present time, one of the most serious problems that face Americans in the area of public policy is the increasing rise in the cost of health care, which has occurred over an extended period of time. One major aspect of the severe crisis in health care costs is that more and more expensive medical technology is being developed and marketed to doctors and hospitals. Even hospitals that are small in size want the latest kind of diagnostic device. The high cost of this expensive equipment is passed on to consumers, who are the patients. It is then passed on to insurance companies. Therefore, many employers are charging their employees more for health insurance because they themselves are having to pay higher and higher premiums. Others are reducing the employees' coverage to a significant extent. Meanwhile, almost forty million Americans suffer from the condition of a lack of any health insurance. In the event that they have an illness or an injury, they must go to a hospital emergency room. In large cities, emergency rooms are being overwhelmed by people seeking treatment for everything from life-threatening gunshot wounds to broken bones.

35.1 Varying sentence length and structure

The following paragraph can be improved by varying sentence length. Read it aloud to get a sense of how it sounds. Then revise it, creating some short sentences and combining other sentences to create more effective long sentences. Feel free to add words or change punctuation. (See *The Everyday Writer,* Chapter 35.)

One way to determine whether a car is a good value is for a consumer to find out if it will be expensive to maintain, for a car that needs frequent repairs will cost more than a car that does not. Prospective buyers can get statistics detailing the number of repairs needed for various makes and models of cars, and that information can be useful. But the number of repairs alone does not tell the whole story about the overall cost of a car's maintenance, as foreign cars may cost more to repair than domestic cars. Routine maintenance such as oil changes can cost more on an import, and parts that have to be ordered from distant places can be quite expensive. A buyer may know the number and cost of repairs of a particular car, yet he or she may still encounter surprises. Sometimes a car that is not an especially reliable model may run for thousands of miles with very little maintenance, and the owner will be delighted. The converse is also true, and sometimes a car from a company with an excellent reputation may be in the shop more than on the road. Consumers are better off doing their homework than trusting to instinct when buying a car, but luck will still play a role.

Sentence Grammar

36.1 Identifying verbs and verb phrases

Underline each verb or verb phrase in the following sentences. (See *The Everyday Writer*, section 36a.) Example:

> Many cultures <u>celebrate</u> the arrival of spring with a festival of some kind.

1. The spring festival of Holi occurs in northern India every March during the full moon.

2. Holi is known as the festival of colors, not only because spring brings flowers but also because Holi celebrations always include brightly colored dyes.

3. According to legend, the festival of colors began thousands of years ago when Krishna played pranks on girls in his village and threw water on them.

4. During Holi, people toss fistfuls of powdered dyes or dye-filled water balloons at each other and sing traditional Holi songs.

5. Holi festivals allow people freedoms that would be unthinkable during the rest of the year.

6. Any person who is walking outside during a Holi celebration will soon be wearing colored powders or colored water.

7. Men, women, and children can throw powders or dye-filled balloons at anyone, even if the person is much older or of much higher status than they are.

8. Some people wear white clothing for Holi.

9. By the end of the celebration, the white clothes are a riot of color.

10. Doesn't Holi sound like fun?

36.2 Identifying nouns and articles

Identify the nouns, including possessive forms, and the articles in each of the following sentences. Underline the nouns once and the articles twice. (See *The Everyday Writer,* section 36b.) Example:

<u><u>The</u> Puritans' hopes</u> were dashed when <u>Charles II</u> regained his <u>father's throne</u>.

1. The squirrel in the front yard seems to have a rat's tail.
2. Slavery existed long before the colonization of America.
3. In the United States at the end of the twentieth century, most people did not own a cell phone, a personal computer, or a digital camera.
4. I chose broccoli over asparagus.
5. Henderson's story is a tale of theft and violation.
6. Doctors are not sure what causes autism.
7. Although plagiarism is dishonest and illegal, it does occur.
8. Nightlife begins in Georgetown even before the sun goes down.
9. In the front row sat two people, a man with slightly graying hair and a young woman in jeans.
10. Journalists should protect their sources except in a serious case in which national security has been compromised.

36.3 Identifying pronouns and antecedents

Identify the pronouns and any antecedents in each of the following sentences, underlining the pronouns once and any antecedents twice. (See *The Everyday Writer*, section 36c.) Example:

A guide <u><u>dog</u></u> must handle <u>itself</u> well in any situation.

1. Everyone has seen a guide dog at some time in his or her life.
2. Guide dogs that work with the blind must act as their human partners' eyes.
3. These dogs learn socialization and basic obedience training when they are puppies.
4. Knowing they will have to give up their dog one day, sighted volunteers agree to live with and train a puppy for the first year of its life.
5. Puppies that are destined to be guide dogs are allowed to go into places that routinely refuse entry to other kinds of dogs.
6. If you see a puppy in a supermarket or an office, look for its special coat that identifies it as a trainee guide dog.
7. Volunteer trainers miss their pups after the training period ends, but nothing is more rewarding than knowing that the pups will make life easier for their new owners.
8. Some of the pups do not pass the requirements to become guide dogs, but these are in great demand as household pets.
9. When a dog passes the test and graduates, it and its blind companion learn to work with each other during an intensive training session.
10. If you are interested in learning about guide dogs or in becoming a volunteer, contact your local school for the blind.

36.4 Identifying adjectives and adverbs

Identify the adjectives and adverbs in each of the following sentences, underlining the adjectives once and the adverbs twice. Remember that articles and some pronouns can function as adjectives. (See *The Everyday Writer*, sections 36d–e.) Example:

> The grand piano waited silently and patiently on the stage.

1. Meerkats are exceptionally social creatures.
2. Politicians must seriously consider how well their lives will withstand intense public scrutiny.
3. Time passed agonizingly slowly, but midnight finally arrived.
4. The shoes in that store are lovely, uncomfortably narrow, and much too expensive.
5. The somewhat shy author spoke reluctantly to six exuberant admirers.
6. We could not resist choosing the smallest and quietest puppy in the litter.
7. The youngest dancer in the troupe performed a brilliant solo.
8. The most instructive of the books is, unfortunately, the longest.
9. Late in the day, the temperature dropped precipitously.
10. Imminent starvation threatens many populations constantly.

36.5 Adding adjectives and adverbs

Expand each of the following sentences by adding appropriate adjectives and adverbs. Delete *the* if need be. (See *The Everyday Writer*, sections 36d–e.) Example:

> Then three   thoroughly   nervous
> ~~The~~ veterinarians examined the patient.
>   ^   ^   ^

46 **Exercises 36.6** *Identifying prepositions*

1. Our assignment is due Wednesday.
2. Most of us enjoy movies.
3. Her superiors praised her work for the Environmental Protection Agency.
4. A corporation can fire workers.
5. The heroine marries the prince.
6. The boardwalk crosses the beach.
7. I have neglected my friend.
8. The media are ignoring his candidacy.
9. Nobody saw the bear, but the ranger said it was dangerous.
10. Which way did you say the pair went?

36.6 Identifying prepositions

Underline the prepositions in the following sentences. (See *The Everyday Writer*, section 36f.) Example:

<u>According to</u> Greek mythology, Cronus presided <u>over</u> the heavens and the earth <u>during</u> the Golden Age.

1. Ares, the god of war, was known for charging into battle without any forethought.
2. Actaeon stumbled upon the pool where Artemis was bathing, and the goddess changed him into a stag as a punishment.
3. Metis turned into a fly and Zeus swallowed her, so she took up residence in his head.
4. Due to Zeus's complaints of constant headaches, Hephaestus split through his skull with an axe.

5. Upon this, Athena emerged, fully grown, from her father's head.

6. In spite of Hera's jealousy, Zeus often came down from Mt. Olympus to visit the mortal women who lived below.

7. Paris sailed across the sea toward Troy out of desire for the beautiful Helen.

8. Huge branches laden with fruit hung above the head of Tantalus, but whenever he reached up to grab them, they moved beyond his reach.

9. In the story of Persephone, Hades tells Demeter that her daughter must live with him beneath the earth for three months each year.

10. From Mt. Olympus, Zeus spied the beautiful Danae, and he descended upon her in the form of a rain shower.

36.7 Identifying conjunctions

Underline the coordinating, correlative, and subordinating conjunctions as well as the conjunctive adverbs in each of the following sentences. Draw a connecting line to show both parts of any correlative conjunctions. (See *The Everyday Writer*, section 36g.) Example:

We used sleeping bags <u>even though</u> the cabin had <u>both</u> sheets <u>and</u> blankets.

1. She loves to run and swim, yet her true passion is tennis.

2. Not only did the friends decide to take a road trip for spring break, but they also found someone to sell them a cheap, used van and camping equipment.

3. Pokey is an outside cat; nevertheless, she greets me at the front door each night as I arrive home.

4. When we arrived at the pond, we saw many children playing there.

5. Either the computer crashed or the power went off; anyway, most of the paper has disappeared.

6. Although I live in a big city, my neighborhood has enough trees and raccoons to make me feel as though I live in the suburbs.

7. Should I have the fish or the chicken?

8. I did not know whether to laugh or cry after I realized my mistake.

9. They laughed until tears rolled down their cheeks, for they had never heard such a funny comedian before.

10. Because the downtown area has many successful businesses, people still want to live inside the city limits.

36.8 Identifying conjunctions and interjections

Underline conjunctions once and interjections twice in each of the following sentences. Write COORD (for coordinating), CORREL (for correlative), or SUBORD (for subordinating) in parentheses after each sentence to indicate the types of conjunctions in use. (See *The Everyday Writer*, sections 36g–h.) Example:

Whoops—when I dropped your teacup, it broke.   (SUBORD)

1. Ah, the enticing aroma of gingerbread always makes me feel as if I should have saved room for dessert!

2. Although I prefer cats, I wouldn't mind getting a dog.

3. Jake and Sandy, Elly and Hank, and Sally Jo and Michael all plan to travel together and attend the conference.

4. I stubbed my toe on the nail after I hit my head on the beam. Ouch!

5. Before you order dessert, make sure you have enough money to cover it.

6. Until I saw that movie, I never thought about daily life at that time.

7. The rain kept me from mowing the lawn, but I didn't really mind.
8. Aha! I always suspected they were planning a surprise party, but now I know for sure.
9. If you save money, you'll feel better both now and later.
10. Our parts shipment did not arrive yesterday, so I cannot fill your order.

36.9 Identifying the parts of speech

For each underlined word in the following sentences, write its part of speech as it is used in the sentence. (See *The Everyday Writer*, sections 36a–h.) Example:

    noun   adj (proper)   adj
Selling is as **American** as **apple** pie.

1. <u>Advertisements</u> clearly <u>and</u> directly reflect our sense of what we want.
2. Almost every advertisement, whether it is <u>selling</u> beer or <u>cosmetics</u>, implies that we choose certain products because we want to feel more <u>attractive</u>.
3. And as the <u>frequency</u> of <u>movie</u> ads and music ads <u>suggests</u>, we <u>also</u> crave diversion: we want entertainment and relief <u>from</u> stress.
4. We can pretend that we live in <u>Middle Earth</u> for a few hours <u>while</u> we watch *The Lord of the Rings* <u>on</u> DVD.
5. <u>And</u> we can appreciate the verbal wit of Eminem even though most of us have <u>not</u> grown up in a <u>Detroit</u> trailer park.
6. <u>In</u> addition, advertisements suggest <u>that</u> we <u>consistently</u> worry about <u>our</u> health.
7. We are <u>frequently</u> instructed to ask <u>our</u> doctors about new pharmaceutical products, whether or not <u>we</u> need them or understand what they <u>do</u>.

8. We <u>also</u> get appeals to <u>safety</u>, such as ads for giant SUVs <u>that</u> supposedly protect drivers from bad weather and allow them to drive up mountainsides.

9. <u>Naturally</u>, the <u>SUV</u> ads don't reveal that we rarely drive them <u>to</u> destinations more <u>exotic</u> than the supermarket.

10. But <u>hey</u>, if we <u>bought</u> only products we really needed and could afford, <u>who</u> knows what would happen to <u>the</u> American economy?

37.1 Identifying subjects and predicates

The following sentences are taken from "A Hanging" and "Shooting an Elephant," two essays by George Orwell. Identify the complete subject and the complete predicate in each sentence, underlining the subject once and the predicate twice. (See *The Everyday Writer*, sections 37a–c.) Example:

<u>They</u> <u>were going to have their bit of fun after all</u>.

1. His mouth slobbered.

2. It was an immense crowd, two thousand at the least and growing every minute.

3. One could have imagined him thousands of years old.

4. In a job like that, you see the dirty work of Empire at close quarters.

5. All this was perplexing and upsetting.

6. The hangman, a gray-haired convict in the white uniform of the prison, was waiting beside his machine.

7. The dog answered the sound with a whine.

8. Would I please come and do something about it?

9. And at that distance, peacefully eating, the elephant looked no more dangerous than a cow.

10. We set out for the gallows.

37.2 Identifying subjects

Identify the complete subject and the simple subject in each sentence. Underline the complete subject once and the simple subject twice. (See *The Everyday Writer*, section 37b.) Example:

In America, <u>the <u>sport</u> of soccer</u> is less popular than it is in other countries around the world.

1. The origins of soccer, also called football, trace back to almost every corner of the globe.

2. Ancient Chinese, Greeks and Romans, as well as South and Central Americans, all played versions of "football."

3. Modern-day soccer really began to develop in England in the late nineteenth century.

4. In 1863, eleven London soccer clubs sent their representatives to the Freemason's Tavern for a meeting.

5. Their intended goal was the establishment of a uniform set of guidelines for the sport.

6. In the minority were the proponents of rugby, who were against rules that forbade ball carrying.

7. They did not ultimately have their way.

8. The historical meeting led to the eventual split between rugby and football and to the founding of the Football Association.

9. The major tournament in professional soccer is the international World Cup, which is held every four years.

10. It is the most widely watched sporting event in the world.

37.3 Identifying predicates

Underline the predicate in the following sentences. Then label each verb as linking (LV), transitive (TV), or intransitive (IV). Finally, label all subject (SC) and object (OC) complements and all direct (DO) and indirect (IO) objects. (See *The Everyday Writer*, section 37c.) Example:

                   TV   DO
The governor of Illinois <u>declared</u> <u>a moratorium on executions in his state</u> in 2000.

1. There were fourteen offenses punishable by death in colonial America.

2. In the 1930s, most Americans still favored capital punishment.

3. However, by the late 1960s, many people in this country found capital punishment unfair and ineffective.

4. Supreme Court justices called capital punishment "cruel and unusual" when they outlawed it in 1972.

5. Most of the justices rejected the method rather than the idea of execution itself.

6. Then, lethal injection was developed as an alternative to older execution methods such as hanging.

7. Support for capital punishment increased dramatically in the 1980s and 1990s with the rising fear of crime.

8. In the past few years, DNA evidence has given more than a hundred prisoners on death row their freedom.

9. Many Americans consider the executions of a few innocent people an acceptable price for capital punishment.

10. In 2004, the United States and China were the only industrialized nations that still used the death penalty.

37.4 Identifying prepositional phrases

Identify and underline all the prepositional phrases. Then choose two of the sentences, and for each, write a sentence that imitates its structure. (See *The Everyday Writer*, section 37d.) Example:

> He glanced <u>about the room</u> <u>with a cocky, crooked grin</u>.
>
> The cat stalked around the yard in her quiet, arrogant way.

1. He decided to travel across the ocean to America in search of a better life.
2. He sailed from Italy in an overcrowded boat, but he was happy to be among his countrymen and women.
3. Upon his arrival in this country, he was taken immediately to Ellis Island.
4. Without any formal education and against all odds, he learned English and prospered in business.
5. Even after sixty years in this country, he is still a proud Italian American.

37.5 Using prepositional phrases

Combine each of the following pairs of sentences into one sentence by using one or more prepositional phrases. (See *The Everyday Writer*, section 37d.) Example:

> Teflon is a slippery material/ ^with ~~It has~~ many industrial and household uses.

Exercises 37.6 Identifying verbal phrases

1. Teflon was invented in 1938. The inventor was Dr. Roy J. Plunkett.
2. Polytetrafluoroethylene (PTFE) is the chemical name. Teflon is the brand name.
3. The benefits of PTFE were immediately obvious. Many scientists understood them.
4. The substance allows food to cook in a pan. The food does not stick.
5. Teflon is not supposed to stick to anything. There is one exception, the pan.
6. Early nonstick cookware coating tended to peel off the surface of the pan. The slightest touch of a metal utensil could remove it.
7. The surface of cookware must be roughened. Then a PTFE primer is applied.
8. The primer holds the PTFE coat in place. A physical bond, not a chemical one, keeps the PTFE on the pan.
9. This slippery substance has kitchen uses. It also protects fabrics from stains.
10. The word *Teflon* can be an adjective. It describes a person who seems to get out of sticky situations easily.

37.6 Identifying verbal phrases

Identify and name each participial phrase, gerund phrase, and infinitive phrase in the following sentences. Identify any sentence in which the verbal phrase acts as the subject of the sentence. (See *The Everyday Writer*, section 37d.) Example:

        ┌──————————— subject ———————————┐
        <u>Inventing a computer that can carry on a conversation</u> is not easy.
        └─gerund─┘

Identifying phrases **37.7** **Exercises** 55

1. The brilliant mathematician Alan Turing predicted in 1950 that people in the year 2000 would have a hard time distinguishing computer chat from human conversation.
2. To check Turing's hypothesis, the annual Loebner competition tests computer programs to determine if any of them can successfully mimic a human conversation.
3. The programs competing for the Loebner prize are called "chatterbots."
4. Programmed for artificial intelligence, the chatterbots are supposed to imitate humans in Internet chat rooms.
5. During the test, human judges trying to tell the machines from human decoys carry on conversations at computer keyboards.
6. Teaching a machine artificial intelligence is extremely difficult.
7. So far, no computer program has managed to win the $100,000 prize.
8. Receiving a $2,000 consolation prize was the best that any program in the competition has been able to do.
9. Most of the computer programs in the competition gave themselves away by using either too much logic or too much gibberish.
10. Surprisingly, every human decoy in the competition has also been accused of being a computer by at least one judge.

37.7 **Identifying prepositional, verbal, absolute, and appositive phrases**

Read the following sentences, and identify and label all the prepositional, verbal, absolute, and appositive phrases. Notice that one kind of phrase may appear within another kind. (See *The Everyday Writer*, section 37d.) Example:

Exercises 37.8 Adding phrases

1. To listen to Patsy Cline is sheer delight.
2. The figure outlined against the sky seemed unable to move.
3. Their tails wagging furiously, the dogs at the shelter worked to win new homes.
4. Jane stood still, her fingers clutching the fence.
5. The moviegoers hissed as the villain enticed the child's dog, a Yorkshire terrier, into his car.
6. Floating on my back, I ignored my practice requirements.
7. His favorite form of recreation was taking a nap.
8. Anna, the leader of the group, was reluctant to relinquish any authority.
9. The sun reflected off the magnificent thunderheads, signaling an approaching storm.
10. Shocked into silence, they kept their gaze fixed on the odd creature.

37.8 Adding prepositional, verbal, absolute, and appositive phrases

Use prepositional, participial, infinitive, gerund, absolute, or appositive phrases to expand each of the following sentences. (See *The Everyday Writer*, section 37d.) Example:

> In response to a vigorous shake, the
> ~~The~~ apples dropped from the limb.
> ^

1. The candidates shook hands with the voters.
2. Teresa looked at her mother.
3. The Sunday afternoon dragged.

4. We were uncertain what to do.

5. Tomás had lost almost all his hair.

6. He wondered about the disappearance.

7. Bandini regretted her crime.

8. The letter lay on the desk.

9. They lived in a trailer.

10. Ten hours of sleep exhausted her.

37.9 Using verbal, absolute, and appositive phrases to combine sentences

Use a participial, infinitive, gerund, absolute, or appositive phrase to combine each of the following pairs of sentences into one sentence. (See *The Everyday Writer*, section 37d.) Example:

> His constant complaining
> ~~He complained constantly. This habit~~ irritated his co-workers.
> ^

1. Ireland is known as the Emerald Isle. It is a magical place to visit.

2. Plan to fly into Dublin. You can backpack your way around the country from there.

3. It is easy to find a central hostel. Consult the Internet or a travel guide before you go.

4. Visit the Ballsbridge area. It is home to foreign embassies and many other sites.

5. Dublin Castle was rebuilt many times over the centuries. It was originally a Viking fortress.

6. The Irish National Gallery is worth checking out for art lovers. It is located at Merrion Square West.

Exercises *Identifying dependent clauses*

7. The James Joyce museum is outside Dublin. It would be a mistake to skip it.

8. You can stand on the Martello Tower in Sandycove. The Irish Sea is in front of it.

9. A long day of sightseeing is tiring. You will have many authentic pubs to choose from.

10. It will be difficult to say good-bye to Dublin. There is much more of the country to explore.

37.10 Identifying dependent clauses

Underline the dependent clauses, and label any subordinating conjunctions and relative pronouns in each of the following sentences. (See *The Everyday Writer*, section 37e.) Example:

       rel pron
The Appalachian Trail, **which stretches from Georgia to Maine,** is over 2,100 miles long.

1. Hikers who attempt to walk the whole length of the Appalachian Trail have to put their lives on hold for several months.

2. Most of these hikers start in Georgia when spring arrives in the South.

3. Hikers have to carry all essentials with them because most of the trail meanders through forested mountains far from any towns.

4. Although the Appalachian mountain range has relatively low peaks, they are still a formidable barrier for foot travelers.

5. If a hilly trek with a forty-pound backpack does not sound like a vacation to you, you probably should think twice about taking on the Appalachian Trail.

Adding dependent clauses 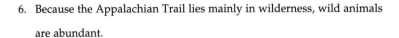 **37.11** Exercises

6. Because the Appalachian Trail lies mainly in wilderness, wild animals are abundant.
7. Many hikers enjoy seeing animals in the wild unless they have a frightening encounter with a bear.
8. Bears that have become accustomed to humans may be a threat to hikers.
9. These bears have learned that people on the Appalachian Trail usually carry plenty of food.
10. Before leaving home, hikers should learn how to react to an aggressive bear to minimize the danger.

37.11 Adding dependent clauses

Expand each of the following sentences by adding at least one dependent clause to it. Be prepared to explain how your addition improves the sentence. (See *The Everyday Writer,* section 37e.) Example:

                who think they are the center of the universe
Spoiled children can drive even their parents crazy.
           ^

1. Working parents may see their children only at the end of the day.
2. Everyone in a family may have high expectations for time together.
3. Children can easily learn how to manipulate their parents.
4. Whining is difficult to listen to and easy to stop with a new toy or an extra video viewing.
5. However, bribing a child to behave better is a flawed technique.
6. Misbehaving children wear out their welcome quickly.
7. Kids should learn that the world does not revolve around their whims.

8. Parents must learn to stick to their own rules.

9. Enforcing rules sometimes worries parents more than it bothers their children.

10. Even if children protest against discipline, they want to know how to behave.

37.12 Distinguishing between phrases and clauses

The following are some sentences from the letters of E. B. White. Read each one carefully, focusing on the phrases and clauses. Underline any dependent clauses once and any phrases twice. Identify each phrase as a prepositional phrase or a verbal phrase. Finally, choose two sentences, and use them as a model for sentences of your own, imitating White's structure phrase for phrase and clause for clause. (See *The Everyday Writer*, sections 37d–e.) Example:

> I was born <u>in 1899</u> and expect <u>to live forever</u>, <u>searching for beauty</u> and <u>raising hell</u> <u>in general</u>.
>
> **PREPOSITIONAL PHRASES:** in 1899, for beauty, in general
> **VERBAL PHRASES:** to live forever, searching for beauty, raising hell
> **IMITATION SENTENCE:** Sarah was hired in May and plans to work all summer, living at home and saving money for law school.

1. Either Macmillan takes Strunk and me in our bare skins, or I want out.

2. I regard the word *hopefully* as beyond recall.

3. Life in a zoo is just the ticket for some animals and birds.

4. I recall the pleasures and satisfactions of encountering a Perelman piece in a magazine.

5. The way to read Thoreau is to enjoy him—his enthusiasms, his acute perception.

6. You can see at a glance that Professor Strunk omitted needless words.

7. A good many of Charlotte's descendants still live in the barn, and when the warm days of spring arrive there will be lots of tiny spiders emerging into the world.

8. When I start a book, I never know what my characters are going to do, and I accept no responsibility for their eccentric behavior.

9. No sensible writer sets out deliberately to develop a style, but all writers do have distinguishing qualities, and they become very evident when you read the words.

10. When I wrote "Death of a Pig," I was simply rendering an account of what actually happened on my place—to my pig, who died, and to me, who tended him in his last hours.

37.13 Classifying sentences grammatically and functionally

Classify each of the following sentences as simple, compound, complex, or compound-complex. In addition, note any sentences that could be classified as declarative, imperative, interrogative, or exclamatory. (See *The Everyday Writer*, section 37f.) Example:

Stop the thief!   simple, imperative

1. During your semester abroad, keep in touch with your family and friends by mail, email, telephone, or even Pony Express if necessary.

2. When I first arrived at college, I became confused about where I fit in and who my role models should be.

3. People go on safari to watch wild animals in their natural habitat.

4. The woman who moved into the apartment next door to mine let her band practice in the living room, but I would not have moved if their music had not been so boring.

Exercises 37.14 *Expressing subjects and objects explicitly*

5. Should he admit his mistake, or should he keep quiet and hope to avoid discovery?
6. The screen door creaked and banged when she ran into the house.
7. Solve your problems yourself.
8. Retail sales declined as consumers cut back on spending, and many small businesses failed.
9. Why do people insist on drinking coffee when tea tastes so much better?
10. Oh, I detest jokes at other people's expense!

37.14 Expressing subjects and objects explicitly

Revise the following sentences or nonsentences so that they have explicit subjects and objects as necessary. If a sentence does not contain an error, write C. (See *The Everyday Writer,* section 37a.) Example:

> It is
> ~~Is~~ easy and convenient for people with access to computers to shop online.

1. No faster way to take care of holiday shopping.
2. Computers also allow people to buy items they cannot find locally.
3. Banks and credit-card companies have websites now, and consumers use for making payments, looking at statements, and transferring balances.
4. Are problems with doing everything online, of course.
5. Customers must use credit cards, and thieves want to break in and get.
6. Are small-time thieves and juvenile pranksters disrupting online services.
7. Jamming popular sites is one way for hackers to gain notoriety, and have been several such actions.

Using noun clauses, infinitives, and gerunds 37.15 Exercises

8. A hacker can get enormous amounts of online data, even if are supposed to be secure.

9. People have every right to be concerned about online privacy, for is a tremendous amount of private information stored in online databases, including medical records and financial data.

10. Internet users must use caution and common sense online, but is also essential for online information to be safeguarded by security experts.

37.15 Using noun clauses, infinitives, and gerunds appropriately

Revise the following sentences as necessary so that each contains an appropriate noun clause, infinitive, or gerund positioned well. If a sentence does not contain an error, write C. (See *The Everyday Writer*, sections 37d–e.) Example:

           that
It pleases me you like me.

1. Is important that we think in English.

2. We discussed to go to a movie, but we could not agree on what to see.

3. It annoys the teacher we don't practice conversation.

4. It is possible that you are right.

5. Ashok refused answering his sister's questions.

6. Her mother stopped to drive on her ninetieth birthday.

7. What he has to say is of great interest to me.

8. It is obvious that she made the right decision.

9. No one expected being allowed to leave work before midnight.

10. We appreciated to get the invitation.

37.16 Using adjective clauses appropriately

Revise the following sentences so that each includes an appropriate adjective clause that is positioned correctly. Make sure the sentence does not include unnecessary words or omit necessary relative pronouns. If a sentence does not contain an error, write C. (See *The Everyday Writer*, section 37e.) Example:

> The student works the hardest gains the most.
> ^who

1. The class has twenty students in it that I am taking.

2. Some students want to practice speaking more asked us all to help prepare a dinner.

3. The class dinner we cooked together represented food from a dozen countries.

4. A reporter attended the dinner and wrote an article which he praised the chefs in it.

5. The chef works at my club helped by lending us pots and pans.

6. My mother makes many delicious dishes that they come from our homeland.

7. She taught me how to make that I have always loved the fritters called *kofte*.

8. We all come from different places, so those of us were cooking together had to speak English to communicate.

9. The room in that we made our dinner smelled delicious.

10. Spoken English, which I had always found very difficult, is easier for me now.

38.1 Using irregular verb forms

Complete each of the following sentences by filling in each blank with the past tense or past participle of the verb listed in parentheses. (See *The Everyday Writer*, section 38c.) Example:

Frida Kahlo ___became___ **(become) one of Mexico's foremost painters.**

1. Frida Kahlo _____ (grow) up in Mexico City, where she _____ (spend) most of her life.

2. She _____ (be) born in 1907, but she often _____ (say) that her birth year _____ (be) 1910.

3. In 1925 a bus accident _____ (leave) Kahlo horribly injured.

4. The accident _____ (break) her spinal column and many other bones, so Kahlo _____ (lie) in bed in a body cast for months.

5. She had always _____ (be) a spirited young woman, and she _____ (take) up painting to avoid boredom while convalescing.

6. Kahlo _____ (meet) the painter Diego Rivera in 1928 and _____ (fall) in love; they married the following year.

7. From the beginning, Rivera had _____ (know) that Kahlo's work was remarkable, so he encouraged her to paint.

8. Kahlo _____ (keep) working even though she _____ (be) in constant pain for the rest of her life.

9. Kahlo usually _____ (choose) to paint self-portraits; scholars have _____ (begin) to analyze her unflinching vision of herself.

10. The fame of Frida Kahlo has _____ (grow) and _____ (spread) since her death in 1954.

38.2 Editing verb forms

Where necessary, edit the following sentences to eliminate any inappropriate verb forms. If the verb forms in a sentence are appropriate as written, write C. (See *The Everyday Writer*, section 38c.) Example:

    chose
He choosed the fish at the restaurant.

1. Be careful not to burnt the toast!
2. She have went to visit her grandparents in Florida.
3. I was so embarrassed that I hunged my head in shame.
4. She thought she was right, but I proved her wrong.
5. James Bond likes his martinis shooken, not stirred.
6. I have always knew you are a good friend.
7. He waked up in totally unfamiliar surroundings.
8. After I swum the race, I was ready for a hearty breakfast.
9. By the time we woke up, the sun had already risen.
10. I wish you had never lend him the money.

38.3 Distinguishing between *lie* and *lay*, *sit* and *set*, *rise* and *raise*

Choose the appropriate verb form in each of the following sentences. (See *The Everyday Writer*, section 38d.) Example:

The boys laid/lay on the couch, hoping for something good on TV.

1. That politician believes people should rise/raise themselves up by their bootstraps.
2. The little girl laid/lay her head on her mother's shoulder, and went to sleep.
3. The students sat/set their backpacks down beside their desks and stared grimly at the new teacher.
4. Sit/Set down and stay awhile.
5. After he died, all the flags were risen/raised to half mast.
6. Don't just lie/lay there; do something!
7. Sitting/Setting in the sun too long can lead to skin cancer.
8. I could really use a rise/raise in pay this time of year.
9. She always lies/lays my fears to rest.
10. As soon as the sun rose/raised, I went for a run.

38.4 Deciding on verb tenses

Complete each of the following sentences by filling in the blank with an appropriate form of the verb given in parentheses. Because more than one form will sometimes be possible, choose one form and then be prepared to explain the reasons for your choice. (See *The Everyday Writer*, section 38e.) Example:

People _have been practicing/have practiced_ **(practice) the art of yoga for thousands of years.**

Exercises 38.4 — Deciding on verb tenses

The present perfect progressive tense *have been practicing* is appropriate because the sentence refers to ongoing action begun in the past and continuing into the present. The present perfect tense *have practiced* is also suitable because it is used to indicate actions begun in the past and either completed at some unspecified time in the past or continuing into the present.

1. The word *yoga* _____ (come) from Sanskrit, one of the world's ancient languages.

2. Although many people today _____ (begin) a yoga practice purely for physical exercise, it is actually a path to spirituality that _____ (date) back thousands and thousands of years.

3. Yoga's popularity in the United States _____ (explode) over the last decade.

4. As a result of this surge in popularity, many yoga studios _____ (open) throughout the city.

5. When you _____ (begin) a yoga practice, it is important to find a reputable teacher who _____ (receive) proper certification.

6. She _____ (look) for a gentle introduction to yoga, so I _____ (suggest) Hatha.

7. The yogi B. K. S. Iyengar _____ (develop) Iyengar yoga in the 1930s, and there _____ (be) many Iyengar institutes throughout the world today.

8. If you _____ (search) for a more vigorous workout, Vinyasa _____ (require) more active movement.

9. The teacher at that studio _____ (be) the best one I _____ (see) yet.

10. I _____ (check) out the class schedule for next week to see if she _____ (teach).

38.5 Sequencing tenses

Change the italicized word or phrase in each of the following sentences to create the appropriate sequence of tenses. If a sentence reads acceptably, write C. (See *The Everyday Writer*, section 38f.) Example:

    have sent
He needs to ~~send~~ in his application before today.
    ^

1. The girls *will have eaten* breakfast before they went running.

2. Until I started knitting again last month, I *have forgotten* how.

3. *Having sung* in the shower, he did not hear the doorbell.

4. After Darius said that he wanted to postpone college, I *am trying* to talk him out of it.

5. Will she see her old boyfriend when she *had come* home at Thanksgiving?

6. I *have imagined* the job would be finished by this point.

7. You *will have finished* your paper by the time the semester ends.

8. When he was twenty-one, he *wanted to have become* a millionaire by the age of thirty.

9. The news had just begun when our power *goes* out.

10. *Working* at the law firm for five years, she was ready for a change.

38.6 Converting the voice of a sentence

Convert each sentence from active to passive voice or from passive to active, and note the differences in emphasis these changes make. (See *The Everyday Writer*, section 38g.) Example:

> **Machiavelli advises the prince to gain the friendship of the people.**
>
> The prince is advised by Machiavelli to gain the friendship of the people.

1. The blog "Talking Points Memo" is maintained by Joshua Micah Marshall.
2. The mouthwatering butter cookies were devoured by the hungry children.
3. Have any goals been scored by the team yet?
4. The last doughnut in the box was eaten by Jerry just a few minutes ago.
5. The experimental data are analyzed in the next section of this report.
6. For months, the baby kangaroo is protected, fed, and taught how to survive by its mother.
7. An American teenager narrates DBC Pierre's prizewinning novel about a Columbine-like school shooting, *Vernon God Little*.
8. The lawns and rooftops were covered with the first snow of winter.
9. The radio reporter advised drivers to avoid the flooded parkway.
10. A lack of customers forced the store to close.

38.7 Using subjunctive mood

Revise any of the following sentences that do not use the appropriate subjunctive verb forms required in formal or academic writing. If the verb forms in a sentence are appropriate as printed, write C. (See *The Everyday Writer*, section 38h.) Example:

>   were
> **I saw how carefully he moved, as if he ~~was~~ caring for an infant.**

1. Even if I was rich, I wouldn't buy those overpriced shoes.

2. The family requested that contributions be made in Gertrude's memory to a Democratic presidential candidate.

3. The lawyer made it seem as if I was a threat to society.

4. Marie would have gone to the Patti Smith show on New Year's Eve if she would have heard about it in advance.

5. I wish I was with you right now.

6. It is necessary that the manager knows how to do any job in the store.

7. Her stepsisters treated Cinderella as though she was a servant.

8. The invisible announcer requested that audience members should not take photographs.

9. The only requirement is that the tense of both clauses makes sense.

10. If more money was available, we would be able to offer more student scholarships.

38.8 Writing conditional sentences

Revise each of the following sentences so that both the *if* clause and the main, or independent, clause contain appropriate verb forms. If a sentence does not contain an error, write C. (See *The Everyday Writer*, section 38h.) Example:

> If you want to work as a computer programmer, you ~~would~~ probably *are* ~~be~~ having a hard time finding a high-paying U.S. job these days.

1. Until recently, many people thought that U.S. computer jobs will go unfilled unless college-educated foreign workers will be allowed to work in this country.

Exercises 38.9 — Using forms of verbs

2. If the dot-com boom had continued, that prediction might come true.

3. Instead, many highly skilled U.S. technology workers will have few options if they became unemployed tomorrow.

4. If any computer job is announced these days, hundreds of qualified people applied for it.

5. Today, if a company uses many programmers or other computer experts, it may hire workers in India to fill the positions.

6. If Indian workers would require as much money as Americans do to live, U.S. companies would not be as eager to outsource computer work to the other side of the world.

7. If business owners cared more about keeping good jobs at home, they hired skilled workers here instead of skilled workers in another country.

8. Will fewer Americans be unemployed right now if the dot-com boom had never happened?

9. Some young people in this country would not have gotten useless technology degrees if they knew how the economy would decline.

10. If American students would want to prepare for a secure future, they should consider a specialty like nursing, in which jobs are available and the work cannot be sent abroad.

38.9 Using the present, the present perfect, and the past forms of verbs

Rewrite the following passage by adding appropriate forms of *have* and main-verb endings or forms for the verbs in parentheses. (See *The Everyday Writer*, Chapter 38.) Example:

I __like__ (like) to try new foods, so I __have eaten__ (eat) in many different kinds of restaurants in my life.

Using specified forms of verbs **38.10** **Exercises** 73

Several times, I _____ (hear) people musing about the bravery of the first person who ever _____ (eat) a lobster. It _____ (be) an interesting question: what do you _____ (think) _____ (make) anyone do such a thing? But personally, I _____ (wonder) all my life about how ancient people _____ (discover) the art of baking bread. After all, preparing a lobster _____ (be) pretty simple in comparison to baking. Bread _____ (feed) vast numbers of people for centuries, so it certainly _____ (be) a more important food source than lobster, too. Those of us who _____ (love) either lobster or bread (or both) _____ (be) grateful to those who _____ (give) us such a wonderful culinary legacy.

38.10 Using specified forms of verbs

Using the subjects and verbs provided, write the specified sentences. (See *The Everyday Writer,* Chapter 38.) Example:

> **subject:** *Bernie* **verb:** *touch*
> **sentence using a present form:** Bernie touches the soft fur.
> **sentence using the auxiliary verb *had*:** Bernie had touched a squid before.

1. subject: *Professor Jones* verb: *teach*

   sentence using a past form:

   sentence using an auxiliary verb + the past participle form:

2. subject: *dogs* verb: *bark*

   sentence using a past form:

   sentence using the auxiliary *were* + the present participle form:

Exercises 38.10 *Using specified forms of verbs*

3. subject: *The student* verb: *dream*

   sentence using a present form:

   sentence using an auxiliary verb + the past participle form:

4. subject: *I* verb: *bring*

   sentence using a past form:

   sentence using the auxiliary *be* + the present participle form:

5. subject: *baby* verb: *sleep*

   sentence using a present form:

   sentence using an auxiliary verb + past participle form:

6. subject: *teenagers* verb: *consume*

   sentence using a past form:

   sentence using the auxiliary verb *were* + the present participle form:

7. subject: *judge* verb: *expect*

   sentence using a present form:

   sentence using an auxiliary verb + the present participle form:

8. subject: *pasta* verb: *steam*

   sentence using a past form:

   sentence using an auxiliary verb + the present participle form:

9. subject: *pilots* verb: *fly*

   sentence using a past form:

   sentence using an auxiliary verb + the present participle form:

10. subject: *hamburger* verb: *taste*

    sentence using a present form:

    sentence using an auxiliary verb + the past participle form:

38.11 Identifying tenses and forms of verbs

From the following list, identify the form of each verb or verb phrase in the sentences. (See *The Everyday Writer*, Chapter 38.)

simple present   past perfect
simple past   present progressive
present perfect   past progressive

Example:

Judge Cohen considered the two arguments.   Simple past

1. Paul is painting the bedroom, and it looks great so far.
2. She was walking to work when the first plane struck the Twin Towers.
3. By the late 1980s, R.E.M. had become a very popular band.
4. She has admired you for years.
5. Just as we took our seats, the movie began.
6. I have attempted that math problem several times now.
7. Paul required special medical attention for years.
8. My mother has driven the same Mazda for ten years.
9. Horror movies rarely make much of an impression on me, but this one has made me afraid to go out to the parking lot.
10. She had forgotten the assignment.

38.12 Using verbs appropriately

Each of the following sentences contains an error with verbs. Revise each sentence. (See *The Everyday Writer*, Chapter 38.) Example:

        could not
Linguists ~~cannot~~ interpret hieroglyphics before they discovered the
       ∧
Rosetta Stone.

Exercises 39.1 Identifying count and noncount nouns

1. A French engineer was finding a stone half-buried in the mud by the Nile River in Egypt in 1799.
2. The Rosetta Stone is cover with inscriptions in three ancient languages.
3. The inscription at the top of the stone written in Egyptian hieroglyphics, or pictographs, while the lower part gives the same information in an ancient Egyptian language called Demotic and in ancient Greek.
4. At that time, scholars were puzzled by hieroglyphics for centuries.
5. Very soon after its discovery, the French have made copies of the stone.
6. A scholar named Jean-François Champollion could understood both ancient Greek and modern Egyptian, known as Coptic.
7. Champollion knew that he can figure out the Demotic script based on his knowledge of Coptic.
8. From the Coptic inscription, he has learned to read the hieroglyphics.
9. The story of the Rosetta Stone is probably more fascinated than the contents of its inscription.
10. The hieroglyphics, Demotic, and Greek texts all are containing a decree from an ancient king.

39.1 Identifying count and noncount nouns

Identify each of the common nouns in the following short paragraph as either a count or a noncount noun. (See *The Everyday Writer*, section 39a.) The first one has been done for you.

      count
In his <u>book</u> *Hiroshima*, John Hersey tells the story of six people who survived the destruction of Hiroshima on August 6, 1945. The bomb detonated at 8:15 in the morning. When the explosion occurred, Mrs. Hatsuyo

Nakamura was looking out her window and watching a neighbor at work on his house. The force of the explosion lifted her into the air and carried her into the next room, where she was buried by roofing tiles and other debris. When she crawled out, she heard her daughter, Myeko, calling out; she was buried up to her waist and could not move.

39.2 Using determiners appropriately; using articles conventionally

Each of these sentences contains an error with a noun phrase. Revise each sentence. (See *The Everyday Writer*, sections 39b–c.) Example:

> Many people use small *a* sponge to clean their kitchen counters.

1. Bacteria are invisible organisms that can sometimes make the people sick.
2. Dangerous germs such as salmonella are commonly found in a some foods.
3. When a cook prepares chicken on cutting board, salmonella germs may be left on the board.
4. Much people regularly clean their kitchen counters and cutting boards to remove bacteria.
5. Unfortunately, a warm, wet kitchen sponge is a ideal home for bacteria.
6. Every time someone wipes a counter with dirty sponge, more germ are spread around the kitchen.
7. Microwaving a dirty sponge for one minute will kill a most bacteria that live in it.
8. According to research studies, the young single men's kitchens tend to have a fewer germs than many other kitchens.

Exercises 39.3 Using articles appropriately

9. These surprising fact tells researchers that young single men do not often wipe their kitchen counters.

10. To eliminate dangerous many bacteria from the kitchen, a cooks should wash their hands frequently.

39.3 Using articles appropriately

Insert articles as necessary in the following passage. If no article is needed, leave the space blank. (See *The Everyday Writer,* section 39c.) Example:

One of ___the___ things that make _____ English unique is ___the___ number of _____ English words.

_____ English language has _____ very large vocabulary. About _____ 200,000 words are in _____ everyday use, and if _____ less common words are included, _____ total reaches more than _____ million. This makes _____ English _____ rich language, but also _____ difficult one to learn well. In addition, _____ rules of English grammar are sometimes confusing. They were modeled on _____ Latin rules, even though _____ two languages are very different. Finally, _____ fact that _____ English has _____ large number of _____ words imported from _____ other languages makes _____ English spelling very hard to master. _____ English is now _____ most widely used language around _____ world, so _____ educated people are expected to know it.

40.1 Selecting verbs that agree with their subjects

Underline the appropriate verb form in each of the following sentences. (See *The Everyday Writer*, Chapter 40.) Example:

Bankers, politicians, and philanthropists alike is/<u>are</u> becoming increasingly interested in microfinance.

1. Many microlending institutions has/have been in existence since the 1970s.
2. In microlending, small loans is/are provided to poor entrepreneurs in developing nations.
3. These borrowers do/does not possess the collateral required for more traditional loans.
4. Many microlenders has/have made women the primary recipients of their loans.
5. Microloans offer/offers more than just a handout; they promote long-term economic development.
6. Bangladeshi economist Muhammad Yunus is/are considered to be one of the pioneers of the microlending revolution.
7. The Grameen Bank, which Yunus founded in 1976, extend/extends banking services to the poor.
8. Yunus, along with Grameen Bank, was/were the recipient of the 2006 Nobel Peace Prize.

9. A recently published list of the greatest entrepreneurs of all time include/includes Bill Gates, Henry Ford, Benjamin Franklin, and Dr. Yunus.

10. These days, everybody has/have the chance to become an investor through Internet microlending organizations.

40.2 Making subjects and verbs agree

Revise the following sentences as necessary to establish subject-verb agreement. If a sentence does not require any change, write C. (See *The Everyday Writer*, Chapter 40.) Example:

                                                             has
A new museum displaying O. Winston Link's photographs ~~have~~ opened in Roanoke, Virginia.

1. Anyone interested in steam locomotives have probably already heard of the photographer O. Winston Link.

2. Imagine that it are the 1950s, and Link is creating his famous photographs.

3. The steam locomotives—the "iron horses" of the nineteenth century—has begun to give way to diesel engines.

4. Only the Norfolk & Western rail line's Appalachian route still use steam engines.

5. Link, a specialist in public relations, is also a commercial photographer and train lover.

6. He and his assistant Thomas Garver sets up nighttime shots of steam locomotives.

7. Days of setup is required for a single flash photo of a train passing by.

8. Many of the photos show scenes that would have been totally in the dark without Link's flashbulbs.

Using subjective case pronouns **41.1** **Exercises**

9. Up to sixteen flashbulbs and specialized reflectors illuminates every important detail.

10. Link's fine photographic eye and his ability to imagine how the flash will look allows him to compose each photo in advance in the dark.

11. His book *Steam, Steel, and Stars* include most of his stunning nighttime train photographs.

12. Famous Link photos, such as one of a steam engine passing a drive-in movie, appear in the book.

13. Today, the photographs of O. Winston Link has a cult following.

14. More than two thousand negatives from the steam locomotive era belongs to the O. Winston Link Museum in Roanoke.

15. Almost everyone who has seen a Link photograph remembers it.

41.1 Using subjective case pronouns

Replace the underlined noun or nouns in each of the following sentences with the appropriate subjective case pronoun. (See *The Everyday Writer*, section 41a.) Example:

       he
Jack and ~~George~~ visited the new science library.

1. The person who got the highest mark on the test was <u>Susan</u>.

2. Due to the inclement weather, <u>Kerry, Jill, and Molly</u> were forced to cancel their trip.

3. As the sun rose that morning, Melina considered how lucky <u>Melina</u> was to be able to see it.

4. As the cattle crossed the road, <u>the cattle</u> stopped all traffic.

5. Whenever Ann and I talk on the phone, it is as if <u>Ann and I</u> are back in high school again.

6. The library has a collection of Mark Twain's manuscripts, but <u>the manuscripts</u> are not available to the general public.

7. Whenever the computer freezes up, <u>the computer</u> has to be restarted.

8. <u>Tina, Rahul, Fredo, and I</u> stayed up all night watching *The Godfather* trilogy.

9. Fredo decided that <u>Fredo</u> did not like the scene where Michael has his own brother killed.

10. The mother felt that <u>her teenagers, Sally and Joe</u>, were watching too much television.

41.2 Using objective case pronouns

Most of the following sentences contain underlined pronouns used incorrectly. Revise the incorrect sentences so that they contain correct objective case pronouns. If a sentence is correct, write C. (See *The Everyday Writer*, section 41a.) Example:

                me
Eventually, the headwaiter told Kim, Stanley, and I̬ that we could be seated.

1. Who do you think is the better tennis player, Mac or <u>he</u>?

2. The president gave <u>her</u> the highest praise.

3. The children wondered which presents under the tree were for <u>themselves</u>.

4. When we asked, the seller promised <u>we</u> that the software would work on our computer.

5. Though even the idea of hang gliding made <u>herself</u> nervous, she gave it a try.

Using possessive case pronouns **41.3** **Exercises** 83

6. The teacher praised <u>they</u> for asking thoughtful questions.

7. Cycling thirty miles a day was triathlon training for Bill, Ubijo, and <u>I</u>.

8. Dennis asked her and <u>me</u> to speak to him in the office.

9. Between you and <u>I</u>, that essay doesn't deserve a high grade.

10. I couldn't tell who was more to blame for the accident, <u>yourself</u> or Susan.

41.3 Using possessive case pronouns

Insert a possessive pronoun in the blank in each sentence. (See *The Everyday Writer*, section 41a.) Example:

<u>My</u> girlfriend bought flowers for me on Valentine's Day.

1. All day long, people in the office asked admiringly, "_____ flowers are those?"

2. I told them the bouquet was _____.

3. The arrangement was perfectly complemented by _____ vase, which my girlfriend had chosen.

4. _____ selection for me was red roses.

5. Every flower has _____ own meaning, according to a Victorian tradition.

6. Roses are easy to understand; _____ meaning is "true love."

7. My girlfriend knows that roses are my favorite flower; _____ are daffodils.

8. I really appreciated _____ going to the trouble and expense of buying me flowers.

9. Not only was it Valentine's Day, but she and I were also celebrating the anniversary of _____ first date.

10. That's the story of my most romantic moment; now tell me _____ .

41.4 Using *who*, *whoever*, *whom*, or *whomever*

Insert *who*, *whoever*, *whom*, or *whomever* appropriately in the blank in each of the following sentences. (See *The Everyday Writer*, section 41b.) Example:

She is someone ___who___ will go far.

1. Professor Quinones asked _____ we wanted to collaborate with.

2. I would appreciate it if _____ made the mess in the kitchen could clean it up.

3. _____ shall I say is calling?

4. Soap operas appeal to _____ is interested in intrigue, suspense, joy, pain, grief, romance, fidelity, sex, and violence.

5. I have no sympathy for _____ was caught driving while intoxicated after the party Friday night.

6. _____ will the new tax law benefit most?

7. The plumbers _____ the landlord hired to install the new toilets in the building have botched the job.

8. She trusted only those _____ were members of her own family.

Using pronouns **41.5** **Exercises** 85

9. _____ did you think deserved the award?

10. The ballroom is available for children's parties or for

    _____ wants to rent it.

41.5 Using pronouns in compound structures, appositives, elliptical clauses; choosing between *we* and *us* before a noun

Choose the appropriate pronoun from the pair in parentheses in each of the following sentences. (See *The Everyday Writer*, sections 41c–e.) Example:

   Of the group, only (<u>she</u>/her) and I finished the race.

1. All the other job applicants were far more experienced than (I/me).

2. Only (he/him) and the two dressmakers knew what his top-secret fall line would be like.

3. When Jessica and (she/her) first met, they despised each other.

4. I know that I will never again love anybody as much as (he/him).

5. To (we/us) New Englanders, hurricanes are a bigger worry than tornadoes.

6. The post-holiday credit card bills were a rude shock to Gary and (she/her).

7. Tomorrow (we/us) raw recruits will have our first on-the-job test.

8. When we heard the good news, we were happy for (they/them) and their children.

9. You may think that Anita will win Miss Congeniality, but in fact, everyone likes you better than (she/her).

10. Keith Richards scoffed at the words "Sir Mick Jagger," but (he/him) and Mick apparently don't agree about knighthood.

11. Just between you and (I/me), this seminar is a disaster!

12. Staying a week in a lakeside cabin gave (we/us) New Yorkers a much-needed vacation.

13. I always thought that my friend Alexis was the smartest of (we/us) all.

14. You might have studied harder than (I/me), but I still received a better grade.

15. Seeing (he and I/him and me) dressed up in her best clothes made Mom laugh until she saw the lipstick on the rug.

41.6 Maintaining pronoun-antecedent agreement

Revise the following sentences as needed to create pronoun-antecedent agreement and to eliminate the generic *he* and any awkward pronoun references. Some sentences can be revised in more than one way, and two sentences do not require any change. If a sentence is correct as written, write *C*. (See *The Everyday Writer*, section 41f.) Example:

Everyone should make his own decision about having children.

Everyone should make his or her own decision about having children.
OR
All individuals should make their own decision about having children.

1. Someone who chooses not to have any children of his own is often known today as "child-free" rather than "childless."

2. A child-free person may feel that people with children see his time as less valuable than their own.

3. Corporate culture sometimes offers parents more time off and other perks than it provides to nonparents.

4. A child-free employee may feel that they have to subsidize family medical plans at work for people who have children.

5. Neither parents nor a child-free person has the right to insist that their childbearing choice is the only correct one to make.

6. However, a community has to consider the welfare of their children because caring for and educating children eventually benefits everyone.

7. Neither an educated citizenry nor a skilled workforce can exist if they are not financed and helped by older generations.

8. Almost no one would be able to afford to have children if they were expected to pay for educating and training their offspring entirely without help.

9. People who feel that they should not have to help pay for quality day care and schools have not thought through their responsibilities and needs as members of society.

10. As writer Barbara Kingsolver once pointed out, in their old age even someone without children will probably need the services of a doctor or a mechanic.

41.7 Clarifying pronoun reference

Revise each of the following sentences to clarify pronoun reference. All the items can be revised in more than one way. If a pronoun refers ambiguously to more than one possible antecedent, revise the sentence to reflect each possible meaning. (See *The Everyday Writer,* section 41g.) Example:

After Jane left, Miranda found her keys.

Miranda found Jane's keys after Jane left.

Miranda found her own keys after Jane left.

Exercises 41.8 Revising to clarify pronoun reference

1. Quint trusted Smith because she had worked for her before.
2. Not long after the company set up the subsidiary, it went bankrupt.
3. When drug therapy is combined with psychotherapy, the patients relate better to their therapists, are less vulnerable to what disturbs them, and are more responsive to them.
4. When Deyon was reunited with his father, he wept.
5. Bill smilingly announced his promotion to Ed.
6. On the weather forecast, it said to expect snow in the overnight hours.
7. The tragedy of child abuse is that even after the children of abusive parents grow up, they often continue the sad tradition of cruelty.
8. Lear divides his kingdom between the two older daughters, Goneril and Regan, whose extravagant professions of love are more flattering than the simple affection of the youngest daughter, Cordelia. The consequences of this error in judgment soon become apparent, as they prove neither grateful nor kind to him.
9. Anna smiled at her mother as she opened the birthday gift.
10. The visit to the pyramids was canceled because of the recent terrorist attacks on tourists there, which disappointed Kay, who had waited years to see them.

41.8 Revising to clarify pronoun reference

Revise the following paragraph to establish a clear antecedent for every pronoun that needs one. (See *The Everyday Writer*, section 41g.)

In Paul Fussell's essay "My War," he writes about his experience in combat during World War II, which he says still haunts his life. Fussell confesses that he joined the infantry ROTC in 1939 as a way of getting out of gym class, where he would have been forced to expose his "fat and flabby" body to the ridicule of his classmates. However, it proved to be a serious miscalculation. After the United States entered the war in 1941, other male college students were able to join officer training programs in specialized fields that kept them out of combat. If you were already in an ROTC unit associated with the infantry, though, you were trapped in it. That was how Fussell came to be shipped to France as a rifle-platoon leader in 1944. Almost immediately they sent him to the front, where he soon developed pneumonia because of insufficient winter clothing. He spent a month in hospitals; because he did not want to worry his parents, however, he told them it was just the flu. When he returned to the front, he was wounded by a shell that killed his sergeant.

42.1 Using adjectives and adverbs appropriately

Revise each of the following sentences to maintain correct adverb and adjective use. Then, for each adjective and adverb you've revised, point out the word that it modifies. (See *The Everyday Writer*, Chapter 42.) Example:

Almost every language ~~common~~ *commonly* uses nonverbal cues that people can interpret.

1. Most people understand easy that raised eyebrows indicate surprise.
2. When a man defiant crosses his arms across his chest, you probably do not need to ask what the gesture means.
3. You are sure familiar with the idea that bodily motions are a kind of language, but is the same thing true of nonverbal sounds?

Exercises 42.2 *Using modifiers appropriately*

4. If you feel sadly, your friends may express sympathy by saying, "Awww."

5. When food tastes well, diners express their satisfaction by murmuring, "Mmmm!"

6. If you feel relievedly that a long day is finally over, you may say, "Whew!"

7. These nonverbal signals are called "paralanguage," and they are quick becoming an important field of linguistic study.

8. Paralanguage "words" may look oddly on paper.

9. Written words can only partial indicate what paralanguage sounds like.

10. Lucky for linguists today, tape recorders are readily available.

42.2 Using comparative and superlative modifiers appropriately

Revise each of the following sentences to use modifiers correctly, clearly, and effectively. A variety of acceptable answers is possible for each sentence. (See *The Everyday Writer,* section 42d.) Example:

> When Macbeth and Lady Macbeth plot to kill the king, she shows herself to be the ~~most~~ *more* ambitious of the two.

1. Some critics consider *Hamlet* to be Shakespeare's most finest tragedy.

2. Romeo and Juliet are probably the famousest lovers in all of literature.

3. The professor who acted out the hero's lines had the most unique teaching style.

4. Did you like the movie *Titus* or the play *Titus Andronicus* best?

5. One of my earlier memories is of seeing my mother onstage.

6. The star of the film is handsome, but he is the worse actor I have ever seen.

7. Shylock is not a likeable character, but he gives a more better speech than anyone else in the play.

8. The film was funny, but I like sad stories more.

9. My classmates and I disagree on which play made a better film: *King Lear*, *Macbeth*, or *Richard III*.

10. Shakespeare supposedly knew little Latin, but most people today know even littler.

42.3 Positioning modifiers

Possible modifiers for each of the following nouns are listed in parentheses after the noun. Indicate the order in which the adjectives should precede the noun. (See *The Everyday Writer,* section 42g.) Example:

Popular New Orleans jazz **album (jazz/New Orleans/popular)**

1. _____ mansion (old/creaky)

2. _____ mining town (uninhabited/dusty/dry)

3. _____ movie (moving/poignant/epic)

4. _____ beach (local/crowded)

5. _____ cloud (threatening/storm)

6. _____ team (coed/volleyball)

7. _____ cloth (batik/orange/unusual)

8. _____ program (educational/worthwhile)

9. _____ pumpkin (orange/fat)
10. _____ rental (movie/X-rated)

43.1 Revising sentences with misplaced modifiers

Revise each of the following sentences by moving any misplaced modifiers so that they clearly modify the words they are intended to. You may have to change grammatical structures for some sentences. (See *The Everyday Writer*, section 43a.) Example:

> Elderly people and students live in the neighborhood
> full of identical tract houses
> surrounding the university/. ~~which is full of identical tract houses.~~

1. Doctors recommend a new test for cancer, which is painless.

2. The tenor captivated the entire audience singing with verve.

3. I went through the process of taxiing and taking off in my mind.

4. The city approximately spent twelve million dollars on the new stadium.

5. Am I the only person who cares about modifiers in sentences that are misplaced?

6. On the day in question, the patient was not normally able to breathe.

7. Refusing to die at the end of the play, the audience stared in amazement at the actor playing Hamlet.

8. The clothes were full of holes that I was giving away.

9. Revolving out of control, the maintenance worker shut down the turbine.

10. A wailing baby was quickly kissed by the candidate with a soggy diaper.

43.2 Revising squinting modifiers, disruptive modifiers, and split infinitives

Revise each of the following sentences by moving disruptive modifiers and split infinitives as well as by repositioning any squinting modifier so that it unambiguously modifies either the word(s) before it or the word(s) after it. You may have to add words to a sentence to revise it adequately. (See *The Everyday Writer*, sections 43a–b.) Example:

The course we hoped would engross us completely bored us.

The course we hoped would completely engross us bored us.
OR
The course we hoped would engross us bored us completely.

1. Airline security personnel asked Ishmael, while he was hurrying to make his connecting flight, to remove his shoes and socks and to open his carry-on bag.
2. He remembered vividly enjoying the sound of Mrs. McIntosh's singing.
3. Bookstores sold, in the first week after publication, fifty thousand copies.
4. The mayor promised after her reelection she would not raise taxes.
5. The exhibit, because of extensive publicity, attracted large audiences.
6. The collector who owned the painting originally planned to leave it to a museum.
7. Doug hoped to perhaps this time succeed in training the cat to stay in one place even when it was not sleeping.
8. Doctors can now restore limbs that have been severed partially to a functioning condition.
9. A new housing development has gone up with six enormous homes on the hill across the road from Mr. Jacoby's farm.

10. The speaker said when he finished he would answer questions.

11. People who swim frequently will improve their physical condition.

12. The compost smelled after a long summer under the blazing sun pretty bad when I turned it.

13. The state commission promised at its final meeting to make its recommendations public.

14. Stella did not want to argue, after a long day at work and an evening class, about who was going to do the dishes.

15. In the next several months, Lynn hopes to despite her busy schedule of entertaining maintain her diet and actually lose weight.

43.3 Revising dangling modifiers

Revise each of the following sentences to correct the dangling modifiers. (See *The Everyday Writer*, section 43c.) Example:

                  a viewer gets
Watching television news, an impression is given of constant disaster.

1. High ratings are pursued by emphasizing fires and murders.

2. Interviewing grieving relatives, no consideration is shown for their privacy.

3. To provide comic relief, heat waves and blizzards are attributed to the weather forecaster.

4. Chosen for their looks, the newscasters' journalistic credentials are often weak.

5. As a visual medium, complex issues are hard to present in a televised format.

6. Assumed to care about no one except Americans, editorial boards for network news shows reject many international stories.
7. Generally only twenty-two minutes long, not including commercials, viewers have little time to absorb information.
8. Horrified by stories of bloodshed, the low probability of becoming the victim of crime or terrorism goes unrecognized.
9. Increasing fears among viewers, Americans worry about unlikely events such as children being kidnapped by strangers.
10. Not covering less sensational but more common dangers such as reckless driving and diabetes, viewers may not understand what is really likely to hurt them.

44.1 Using prepositions idiomatically

Insert one or more appropriate prepositions in each of the following sentences. (See *The Everyday Writer*, section 44a.) Example:

We will have the answer ___by___ four o'clock this afternoon.

1. Shall we eat _____ the restaurant, or would you prefer to take food _____?
2. I hate driving _____ the city _____ rush hour.
3. Have you ever fallen _____ love at first sight?
4. To get to my house, drive _____ Valley Road and make a right _____ Cherry Street.
5. Adults who read to children can provide good examples _____ them.

6. Students should get to school precisely _____ time.

7. Having someone to help them _____ home gives struggling students more confidence.

8. Schools themselves may be struggling _____ financial cutbacks and poor facilities.

9. Classrooms need books _____ their shelves.

10. A high-quality public education should be given _____ every child.

44.2 Recognizing and using two-word verbs

Identify each italicized expression as either a two-word verb or a verb + preposition. (See *The Everyday Writer,* section 44b.) Example:

Look *up* John Brown the next time you're in town.   two-word verb

1. George was still *looking for* his keys when we left.

2. I always *turn down* the thermostat when I go to bed or leave the house.

3. We drank a pitcher of lemonade in an attempt to *cool* ourselves *off* on a sweltering July afternoon.

4. Marion *gave back* the ring she had gotten as an engagement gift.

5. Jimmy *takes after* his father, poor thing.

6. The car *turned into* the driveway.

7. The frog *turned into* a prince.

8. The camp counselor *handed* the candy *out* as if it were gold.

9. *Put* the garbage *out* on the sidewalk, please.

10. Don't *put* yourself *out* on my behalf.

45.1 Revising comma splices and fused sentences

Revise each of the following comma splices or fused sentences by using the method suggested in brackets after the sentence. (See *The Everyday Writer*, Chapter 45.) Example:

Americans think of slavery as a problem of the pastˌ but it still exists in some parts of the world. [Join with a comma and a coordinating conjunction.]

1. We tend to think of slavery only in U.S. terms in fact, it began long before the United States existed and still goes on. [Separate into two sentences.]

2. The group Human Rights Watch filed a report on Mauritania, it is a nation in northwest Africa. [Recast as one independent clause.]

3. Slavery has existed in Mauritania for centuries it continues today. [Join with a comma and a coordinating conjunction.]

4. Members of Mauritania's ruling group are called the Beydanes, they are an Arab Berber tribe also known as the White Moors. [Recast as one independent clause.]

5. Another group in Mauritania is known as the Haratin or the Black Moors, they are native West Africans. [Separate into two sentences.]

6. In modern-day Mauritania many of the Haratin are still slaves, they serve the Beydanes. [Join with a semicolon.]

7. The first modern outcry against slavery in Mauritania arose in 1980, protesters objected to the public sale of an enslaved woman. [Recast as an independent and a dependent clause.]

Exercises 45.1 — Revising comma splices and fused sentences

8. Mauritania outlawed slavery in 1981 little has been done to enforce the law. [Join with a comma and a coordinating conjunction.]

9. The law promised slaveholders financial compensation for freeing their slaves however, the language of the law did not explain exactly who would come up with the money. [Join with a semicolon.]

10. Physical force is not usually used to enslave the Haratin, rather, they are held by the force of conditioning. [Separate into two sentences.]

11. In some ways the Mauritanian system is different from slavery in the United States, there are few slave rebellions in Mauritania. [Join with a comma and a coordinating conjunction.]

12. By some estimates 300,000 former slaves still serve their old masters these slaves are psychologically and economically dependent. [Recast as an independent and a dependent clause.]

13. Many Mauritanian freed slaves live in their own houses, they may work for their former masters in exchange for a home or for food or medical care. [Recast as an independent and a dependent clause.]

14. In addition, there may be as many as 90,000 Haratin still enslaved, some Beydanes have refused to free their slaves unless the government pays compensation. [Join with a semicolon.]

15. Some Mauritanians claim that slavery is not a problem in their country in fact, in 2001, a Mauritanian official told a United Nations committee that slavery had never existed there. [Join with a dash.]

16. Of course, slavery must have existed in Mauritania there would have been no compelling reason to make a decree to abolish it in 1981. [Join with a comma and a coordinating conjunction.]

17. The president of Mauritania insisted in 1997 that discussions of modern slavery were intended only to hurt the country's reputation his comments did not offer much hope for opponents of slavery. [Recast as an independent and a dependent clause.]

18. Both the slaveholding Beydanes and the enslaved Haratin are made up largely of Muslims, some people in Mauritania see resistance to slavery in their country as anti-Muslim. [Join with a comma and a coordinating conjunction.]

19. In some cases, Western opponents of Mauritanian slavery may indeed harbor anti-Muslim sentiments that does not justify allowing the slavery to continue. [Join with a semicolon.]

20. Islamic authorities in Mauritania have agreed that all Muslims are equal therefore, one Muslim must not enslave another. [Join with a semicolon.]

45.2 Revising comma splices

Revise the following paragraph, eliminating all comma splices by using a period or a semicolon. Then revise the paragraph again, this time using any of these three methods:

Separate independent clauses into sentences of their own.

Recast two or more clauses as one independent clause.

Recast one independent clause as a dependent clause.

Comment on the two revisions. What differences in rhythm do you detect? Which version do you prefer, and why? (See *The Everyday Writer*, Chapter 45.)

My sister Julie is planning a spring wedding, obviously she is very excited. At first, she hoped for a simple affair, in fact, she wanted to elope with her fiancé, Mike. My mother was not happy about that, neither was Mike's mother.

Julie agreed to a small party, however, it soon began to grow and grow. Julie decided to invite all her college roommates, also Mike wanted his boss and her husband to attend. The simple arrangement of roses she picked out quickly became an elaborate bundle of rare orchids, the DJ somehow turned into a full live band. The intimate restaurant she first chose could not hold all the guests, now she had to find a new venue. Julie and Mike were growing increasingly anxious, at the same time they were reluctant to disappoint their families. They finally decided on a small ceremony in the backyard for family members only, then a gigantic party afterward for family, friends, and co-workers. I can't wait to see my sister on the special day, she is going to be a beautiful and happy bride!

45.3 Revising comma splices and fused sentences

Revise the following paragraph, eliminating the comma splices and fused sentences by using any of these methods:

Separate independent clauses into sentences of their own.

Link clauses with a comma and a coordinating conjunction.

Link clauses with a semicolon and, perhaps, a conjunctive adverb or a transitional phrase.

Recast two or more clauses as one independent clause.

Recast one independent clause as a dependent clause.

Link clauses with a dash.

Then revise the paragraph again, this time eliminating each comma splice and fused sentence by using a different method. Decide which paragraph is more effective, and why. Finally, compare the revision you prefer with the revisions of several other students, and discuss the ways in which the versions differ in meaning. (See *The Everyday Writer*, Chapter 45.)

A "Sweet 16" has traditionally been viewed as a milestone birthday in our culture, these days it takes on added significance as the year of the driver's license. Many children dream of the freedom and adventure such newfound mobility will afford them they take the driving test the moment they are able. Unfortunately, there is a dark side to teenage driving, namely it is the issue of teens driving while drinking. By some estimates, roughly one out of four 15- to 20-year-olds killed in automobile crashes had been drinking alcohol undoubtedly there are many reasons for this lethal combination. First of all, inexperienced drivers are also inexperienced drinkers they do not yet fully understand the deleterious effect that alcohol can have on them. Teenagers who have been drinking are less likely to use seatbelts, this makes for a greater likelihood of a fatality in the case of an accident. Statistically, teenage drivers who have been drinking often drive too fast, with too many friends in the car, and with the music turned up loud this is the recipe for tragedy. It is not enough for parents and educators to simply tell teenagers not to drink and drive, more definitive action needs to be taken. Groups like Mothers Against Drunk Driving (MADD) work to help educate teenagers and parents about the harmful effects of drinking while driving law enforcement officials are stepping up patrols and checkpoints during holidays notorious for alcohol consumption. Some groups even look to the day when technology will allow a vehicle to recognize a drunk driver the car will not be able to function in such a situation. In the meantime, what teen drivers need most of all are parents who vigilantly make sure their children are sober when they get behind the wheel, they also need parents who are good role models.

46.1 Eliminating sentence fragments

Revise each of the following fragments, either by combining fragments with independent clauses or by rewriting them as separate sentences. (See *The Everyday Writer*, Chapter 46.) Example:

> **Zoe looked close to tears. Standing with her head bowed.**
>
> Standing with her head bowed, Zoe looked close to tears.
>
> Zoe looked close to tears. She was standing with her head bowed.

1. Autumn is a season of lavish bounty and stunning natural beauty. A season of giving thanks.

2. September is the perfect time to run outdoors. Avoiding the need to wait for a treadmill at a crowded gym.

3. To carve pumpkins and see scary movies. What better month than October?

4. For new college students who live on campus, the Columbus Day weekend often marks the first visit back home. For others, Thanksgiving. In any case, the event is often emotionally charged for both parents and students alike.

5. We decided to go camping one weekend in October. Pitching tents and setting up camp.

6. I can't tell if he is skipping the Halloween party because he is genuinely ill. Or if he just doesn't have an idea for a costume.

7. Turning the clocks back one hour in November. In theory, this makes better use of daylight.

8. My sister and her husband are hosting Thanksgiving dinner at their house this year. With Christmas at my parents' house and New Year's Eve at my cousin's. It should be a busy holiday season!

9. Your dreamy stuffing with cornbread, sausage, and sage. Please share the recipe with me!

10. Autumn often begins with hot, summerlike weather. Sometimes warm enough to go swimming outdoors! And by the end of the season, people are shoveling out their driveways and replacing flip-flops with snow boots.

46.2 Revising a paragraph to eliminate sentence fragments

Underline every fragment you find in the following paragraph. Then revise the paragraph. You may combine or rearrange sentences as long as you retain the original content. (See *The Everyday Writer*, Chapter 46.)

To study abroad or not. That is a major decision for many college students. Some will consider domestic programs at universities across the country. Traditionally, approaching their junior year. Opportunities for study in major cities and in small villages. Programs to satisfy every interest and major. While some are reluctant to leave behind the familiar comforts of college life, others look forward. To untold adventure and newfound freedom in exciting new environments. There's a lot to think about. Applications, courses, airfare, accommodations, and visas. Even though students yearn for the experience of studying abroad. Or outside their home university. Those who accept the challenge are generally rewarded. With a once-in-a-lifetime opportunity. Students who travel to foreign destinations can thoroughly immerse themselves in the culture, language, traditions, and foods of their host country. And end up with new friends, an enhanced résumé, and a sense of self-reliance. Why not check with your college today? To see what kinds of foreign and domestic study programs you might apply to.

46.3 Understanding intentional fragments

Choose a newspaper or magazine advertisement that contains intentional fragments. Rewrite the advertisement to eliminate all sentence fragments. Be prepared to explain how your version and the original differ in impact and why you think the copywriters for the ad chose to use fragments rather than complete sentences. (See *The Everyday Writer,* Chapter 46.)

Punctuation and Mechanics

47.1 Using a comma to set off introductory elements

In the following sentences, add any commas that are needed after the introductory element. (See *The Everyday Writer*, section 47a.) Example:

> The inventor of pasteurization, Louis Pasteur was born in France in 1822.

1. Named after its inventor pasteurization is the process of heating liquids in order to destroy viruses and harmful bacteria.

2. Unlike sterilization pasteurization does not destroy all the pathogens in a food.

3. Instead pasteurization tries to reduce the number of all living organisms so they cannot cause illness.

4. While there are many methods of pasteurization the most commonly used is called HTST (for High Temperature/Short Time).

5. Although there are many foods and beverages that are pasteurized we generally think of the process in relation to dairy products.

6. Concerned about the helpful bacteria killed in the pasteurization process some people recommend drinking raw milk.

7. In addition raw milk advocates feel that modern cow breeds consume far too many antibiotics.

8. In stark contrast to their "mainstream" counterparts cows on raw milk dairy farms are not fed commercial feed.

9. Disturbed by the growing popularity of raw milk as a health food some doctors are speaking out in favor of mandatory pasteurization regulations.

10. Whatever your opinion on this issue it is unlikely that the debate will be settled soon.

47.2 Using a comma in compound sentences

Use a comma and a coordinating conjunction (*and, but, or, for, nor, so,* or *yet*) to combine each of the following pairs of sentences into one sentence. Delete or rearrange words if necessary. (See *The Everyday Writer*, section 47b.) Example:

> There is a lot of talk these days about computer viruses. Many people do not know what they really are.
>
> *, yet many* (replacing ". Many")

1. Computer viruses are software programs. They are created to spread from one computer to another.

2. A biological virus cannot replicate itself. A virus must inject its DNA into a cell in order to reproduce.

3. Similarly, a computer virus must hitch on to some other computer program. Then it can launch itself.

4. These viruses can be totally destructive or basically benign. When people think of computer viruses, they generally think of the former.

5. Most viruses spread easily via attachments or instant messaging. One should never open an email attachment unless he or she knows the sender.

6. Viruses can be distributed through downloads. They can be spread through black-market software.

7. Computer users should not forget about installing a firewall to protect themselves. They should not ignore their computer's prompts to update security.

8. Children love to download computer games from sites they might be unfamiliar with. Parents and teachers should teach children about computer security.

9. Computer security protects the computer. It also protects the children.

10. The world of computer viruses might seem daunting. By following a few basic safety rules, computer users can largely protect themselves.

47.3 Recognizing restrictive and nonrestrictive elements

First, underline the restrictive or nonrestrictive elements in the following sentences. Then, use commas to set off the nonrestrictive elements in the sentences that contain such elements. (See *The Everyday Writer*, section 47c.) Example:

> My only novel, *The Family Kurasch*, is out of print.

1. Anyone who is fourteen years old faces strong peer pressure every day.
2. Embalming is a technique that preserves a cadaver.
3. The word *chortle* which was invented by Lewis Carroll is a combination of the words *chuckle* and *snort*.
4. The girl standing in the hall outside the classroom is protesting the new rule on school prayer.
5. You should get a carbon monoxide detector if you have a fireplace.
6. My favorite pastime reading web logs often prevents me from getting enough sleep or doing all my homework.
7. Birds' hearts have four chambers whereas reptiles' have three.

Exercises 47.4 Using commas to set off items in a series

8. Karl Marx an important nineteenth-century political philosopher believed that his role as a social thinker was to change the world.

9. The president elected for a six-year term acts as head of state.

10. The Zuñis an ancient tribe live in New Mexico.

11. Thurgood Marshall the first African American to serve on the U.S. Supreme Court died in 1993.

12. Houses made of wood can often survive earthquakes.

13. Trey Parker and Matt Stone who created *South Park* met as college students in Colorado.

14. The man who rescued her puppy won her eternal gratitude.

15. The tornado which had spared Waterville leveled Douglastown.

47.4 Using commas to set off items in a series

In the following sentences, add any commas that are needed to set off words, phrases, or clauses in a series. If no comma is needed, write C. (See *The Everyday Writer*, section 47d.) Example:

The waiter brought water, menus, and an attitude.
                            ^   ^

1. I am very excited to see Alcatraz visit Chinatown and tour Napa Valley.

2. I am looking forward to turning eighteen being able to vote and perhaps serving in the military.

3. The spider's orange body resembles a colored dot amidst eight long black legs.

4. The moon circles the earth the earth revolves around the sun and the sun is just one star among many in the Milky Way galaxy.

5. The ball sailed over the fence across the road and through the Wilsons' window.

6. He is a brilliant demanding renowned concert pianist.

7. They found employment in truck driving farming and mining.

8. My top three favorite nineties bands are Pearl Jam Nirvana and Soundgarden, in that order.

9. Joan is a skilled human resource manager.

10. Superficial observation does not provide accurate insight into people's lives—how they feel what they believe in how they respond to others.

47.5 Using commas to set off parenthetical and transitional expressions, contrasting elements, interjections, direct address, and tag questions

Revise each of the following sentences, using commas to set off parenthetical and transitional expressions, contrasting elements, interjections, words used in direct address, and tag questions. (See *The Everyday Writer*, sections 47e–f.) Example:

Ladies and gentlemen, thank you for your attention.

1. Ouch that tetanus shot really hurt!

2. Doctor Ross you are over an hour late for our appointment.

3. Consider furthermore the impact of environmental destruction on future generations.

4. The West in fact has become solidly Republican in presidential elections.

5. Last year I am sorry to say six elms had to be destroyed.

6. Captain Kirk I'm a doctor not a madman.

7. The celebration will alas conclude all too soon.

Exercises 47.6 Using commas with dates

8. One must consider the society as a whole not just its parts.

9. You didn't really think I would fall for that trick did you?

10. Mary announced, "Kids I want you to clean your rooms not make a bigger mess."

47.6 Using commas with dates, addresses, titles, numbers, and quotations

Revise each of the following sentences, using commas appropriately with dates, addresses and place-names, titles, numbers, and quotations. If no comma is needed in a sentence, write C. (See *The Everyday Writer*, sections 47g–h.) Example:

The wine store's original location was 2373 Broadway, New York City.
                                                       ^

1. "Education is not the filling of a pail, but the lighting of a fire" said William Butler Yeats.

2. I agree with Groucho Marx that "humor is reason gone mad."

3. "The public be damned!" William Henry Vanderbilt was reported to have said. "I'm working for my stockholders."

4. "Who can match the desperate humorlessness of the adolescent who thinks he is the first to discover seriousness?", asks P. J. Kavanaugh.

5. 1600 Pennsylvania Avenue Washington DC is a familiar address to many.

6. On July 21 1969 Neil Armstrong became the first person to walk on the moon.

7. On the tomb, under the name *Rev. Martin Luther King Jr.*, is a quotation from a famous speech: "Free at last! Free at last! Thank God Almighty, we are free at last."

8. "Neat people are lazier and meaner than sloppy people" according to Suzanne Britt.

9. Ithaca New York has a population of about 30000.

10. In my dictionary, the rules of punctuation begin on page 1560.

47.7 Eliminating unnecessary commas

Revise each of the following sentences, deleting unnecessary commas. If a sentence contains no unnecessary commas, write C. (See *The Everyday Writer*, section 47j.) Example:

Insomniacs are people/ who have a hard time sleeping soundly.

1. Contrary to popular belief, insomnia is not simply a matter, of being unable to sleep well at night.

2. Insomniacs do indeed wake up at night, but, studies have demonstrated that they also have trouble napping during the day.

3. Why can't insomniacs sleep soundly at night, or nap when they are tired?

4. In many cases, insomniacs suffer, from anxiety.

5. Doctors and sleep researchers, have long considered anxiety to be a common result of getting too little sleep.

6. However, recent studies indicate that anxiety contributes to sleeplessness, not the other way around.

7. Therapies to help insomniacs, include behavior modification and sleeping pills.

8. Sleep therapists recommend, going to bed at the same time every night, not watching television in bed, and not reading in bed.

Exercises

48.1 Using semicolons to link independent clauses

9. Restless, disturbed, sleep habits are certainly irritating, but are they also, bad for an insomniac's health?

10. While tired people are more dangerous drivers, and less productive workers, no one knows for certain, if insomnia can actually make them sick.

48.1 Using semicolons to link independent clauses

Combine each of the following pairs of sentences into one sentence by using a semicolon. (See *The Everyday Writer*, section 48a.) Example:

Take the bus to Henderson Street; meet me under the clock.

1. Property values in that town have soared. As a result, new residents are increasingly affluent.

2. Teenagers today don't spend all their time on the telephone. Instead, they go online and send each other instant messages.

3. Voltaire was concerned about the political implications of his skepticism. He warned his friends not to discuss atheism in front of the servants.

4. She was distressed about his failing grade in English. On the other hand, she was thrilled about his A in math.

5. Current celebrities don't have to make fools of themselves on reality television shows. Former celebrities jump at the chance.

6. Smith Street in Brooklyn is a popular area filled with restaurants and shops. Many visitors to New York City now include it on their sightseeing itineraries.

7. I used to see nothing but woods when I looked out my back window. The view was nothing like it is now, a treeless expanse of new houses.

8. Establishing your position in an office is an important task. Your profile will mold your relationships with other staff members.

9. *Propaganda* is defined as the spread of ideas to further a cause. Therefore, *propaganda* and *advertisement* are synonyms.

10. That resort is ideal for beginner skiers. In addition, it offers snowboarding classes.

48.2 Revising misused semicolons

Revise each of the following sentences to correct the misuse of semicolons. If the semicolon in a sentence is appropriate as written, write C. (See *The Everyday Writer*, section 48c.) Example:

The new system would encourage high school students to take more academic courses/, thus strengthening college preparation.

1. To make the tacos, I need to buy; ground beef, beans, and tortillas.

2. Verbal scores have decreased by more than fifty-four points; while math scores have decreased by more than thirty-six.

3. For four glorious but underpaid weeks; I'll be working in Yosemite this summer.

4. Finally, I found her at the Humane Society; a beautiful shepherd-collie mix who likes children and plays well with cats.

5. If the North had followed up its victory at Gettysburg more vigorously; the Civil War might have ended sooner.

6. He enjoys commuting to work on the train; although it can get crowded at rush hour.

7. Some gardeners want; low-maintenance plants, limited grass to mow, and low water usage.

Exercises

49.1 Using periods appropriately

8. She dozed off through most of her art history lectures; as a result, she is in danger of failing the course.

9. After school; many fourteen-year-olds head to the mall; where they spend the rest of the day.

10. I will meet you at the movies; as soon as I finish writing my term paper.

49.1 Using periods appropriately

Revise each of the following items, inserting periods in the appropriate places and eliminating any inappropriate punctuation. If a sentence is correct as written, write C. (See *The Everyday Writer*, section 49a.) Example:

> **Dr.** Sarah Blaffer Hrdy has been studying the maternal instinct in humans and other animals.

1. Dr Hrdy, an anthropologist, has studied primate motherhood for many years.

2. She has raised disturbing questions about why parents sometimes kill their offspring?

3. Parents since the Neolithic period of 10,000 BCE have delayed naming infants or otherwise committing to raising them until a few days after birth.

4. Human parents, even in recent centuries, may actively or passively have limited their children's chances to grow up!

5. Dr Hrdy believes that parents may commit infanticide in order to give their other children a better chance

6. The term "parent-offspring conflict" was coined by Robert Trivers, PhD.

7. The popular view of motherhood is that mothers always love their children unconditionally

8. Many mothers are indeed willing to put up with a great deal from their children, from 2.00 A.M. feedings through requests for college tuition.

9. Dr Hrdy asks whether the "maternal instinct" is really instinctive?

10. Describing a mother's crime against her child as "inhuman" is neither accurate nor helpful in preventing future tragedies!

49.2 Using question marks appropriately

Revise each of the following sentences, adding question marks, substituting question marks for other punctuation where appropriate, and removing inappropriately placed question marks. Some sentences do not require any question marks; for those sentences, write C. (See *The Everyday Writer*, section 49b.) Example:

She asked the travel agent, "What is the airfare to Greece?"

1. I couldn't tell if she was offended by my remarks or amused by them?

2. "Which Harry Potter book did you like best," Georgia asked Harriet?

3. I couldn't stop thinking about my choices after graduation: Should I get an entry-level job at a Fortune 500 company. Go to law school. Teach English at an inner-city high school?

4. "Who wants to go to the pool with me" asked May?

5. Liam asked his mother if he could go with his friends to the concert?

6. She wondered if he would ever call back.

7. Do you remember who said, "Be the change you want to see in the world?"

8. We began to ask what might fix the problem—restarting the computer, closing other programs, using a different browser.

9. Is your favorite Springsteen song "Atlantic City"?

10. I asked her if she would be much longer in the bathroom?

49.3 Using exclamation points appropriately

Revise each of the following sentences, adding or deleting exclamation points as necessary and removing any other inappropriate punctuation that you find. (See *The Everyday Writer*, section 49c.) Example:

> Look out~~,~~ ^!^ ~~the~~ ^The^ tide is coming in fast~~,~~ ^!^

1. The defendant stood up in the witness box and shouted, "I didn't do it. You've got to believe me."
2. Oh, no. We've lost the house.
3. The child cried, "Ouch" as her mother pulled off the bandage!
4. "Go! Go! Go!," roared the crowd as the quarterback sped toward the end zone.
5. What, exactly, do you want!?
6. It was an ordinary school day, so the child once again came home to an empty house!
7. Stop, thief.
8. She exclaimed, "It's too hot."
9. The only thing the surprised guest of honor could say was, "Well, I'll be!".
10. "This is ridiculous," sputtered the diner as the waiter brought the wrong order again!

50.1 Using apostrophes to signal possession

Complete each of the following sentences by inserting 's or an apostrophe alone to form the possessive case of the italicized words. (See *The Everyday Writer*, section 50a.) Example:

> Many Internet scare stories are nothing but old *wives*' tales.

1. Internet rumors circulate widely because of *people* good intentions.
2. Recipients who pass on messages want everyone to hear about a *child* inspiring fight against cancer or about some dangerous drug, product, or disease.
3. The *Internet* power to inform is great, but so is its power to play tricks on unsuspecting people.
4. A *hoax* creators count on *recipients* kind hearts and concern for the well-being of their families and friends.
5. *Consumers* fears fuel some of the Internet medical scares.
6. Have you heard the one about how *deodorants* ingredients supposedly clog your pores and cause cancer?
7. Another scare warned that sugar substitutes caused the *body* immune system to malfunction.
8. Some of these scares are probably intended to damage certain *corporations* reputations by spreading rumors about products.
9. Others, like the one about checking your toilet seat to be sure it has not become a deadly *spider* hiding place, probably begin as jokes.
10. The *Internet* speed has made such anonymous rumors spread more rapidly than anyone would have thought possible twenty years ago.

50.2 Using apostrophes to create contractions

Revise each of the following sentences so that it uses contractions. Remove any misused apostrophes. (See *The Everyday Writer*, section 50b.) Example:

> I'll
> ~~I will~~ bring some meatballs to the potluck dinner.

1. He does not know how to get to the library, because he has not ever been there before.

118 Exercises **51.1** *Using quotation marks to signal direct quotations*

2. I will not be able to go swimming this afternoon if it is pouring.

3. I am hungry; let us eat!

4. He is the valedictorian for the class of 2008.

5. For the test you will be taking on Monday, you are required to have a pencil with No. 2 lead.

6. The clothes that I am washing now did not really get too dirty.

7. The caller says he has been waiting an hour for his pizzas, but we do not have any record of his order.

8. The distributor says that your order has not received it's approval from the business office.

9. It is true that a snake can shed it's own skin and can swallow much of it's prey whole.

10. Is not that the new jazz club that is open on weekends?

51.1 Using quotation marks to signal direct quotations

In the following sentences, add quotation marks each time someone else's exact words are being used. Some sentences do not require quotation marks; mark correct sentences C. (See *The Everyday Writer*, section 51a.) Example:

"Your phone's ringing!" yelled Phil from the end of the hall.

1. Dr. King was quoting an old African American spiritual when he said, Free at last! Free at last! Thank God Almighty, we are free at last.

2. My mother told us we had to get in the car immediately or she wouldn't drive us.

3. It's not fair, she told him. You always win.

4. To paraphrase his words, "the planet is in deep trouble if we don't start reducing carbon emissions."

5. Call me Ishmael is the first sentence of novelist Herman Melville's *Moby-Dick*.

6. Most people like to think of themselves as open-minded and flexible enough to change when the circumstances demand.

7. After repeating I can't hear you with her fingers stuck in her ears, Hannah ran to her room and slammed the door.

8. I could not believe the condition of my hometown, he wrote.

9. Keep your opinions to yourselves, Dad muttered as he served the lumpy oatmeal.

10. Is the computer plugged in? the technical support operator asked, prompting Harry to snarl, Yes, I'm not a complete idiot.

51.2 Using quotation marks for titles and definitions

Revise each of the following sentences by using quotation marks appropriately to signal titles and definitions. (See *The Everyday Writer*, sections 51c–d.) Example:

The Chinese American businessman surprised his guest by using the Hebrew word *shalom*, which means "peace."

1. The slogan for the Center for a New American Dream is appropriately simple: More Fun, Less Stuff.

2. My dictionary defines *isolation* as the quality or state of being alone.

3. Two *ER* episodes, Chaos Theory and Freefall, featured Dr. Romano having a run-in with a helicopter.

4. Kowinski uses the term *mallaise* to mean physical and psychological disturbances caused by mall contact.

5. In Flannery O'Connor's short story *Revelation*, colors symbolize passion, violence, sadness, and even God.

6. "The little that is known about gorillas certainly makes you want to know more," writes Alan Moorehead in his essay A Most Forgiving Ape.

7. The British, the guide told us, knit sweaters for their teapots.

8. If you had ever had Stairway to Heaven running through your head for four days straight, you would not like Led Zeppelin either.

9. Big Bill, a section of Dos Passos's book *U.S.A.*, opens with a birth.

10. Amy Lowell challenges social conformity in her poem Patterns.

51.3 Using quotation marks appropriately

Revise each of the following sentences, deleting quotation marks used inappropriately, moving those placed incorrectly, and changing wording as necessary. (See *The Everyday Writer*, Chapter 51.) Example:

Do advertisements /really/ have something to teach us about our culture?

1. Cable channels like "Nickelodeon" include what they term "classic" commercials as part of the programming.

2. Television commercials have frequently used "popular" songs as an effective way to connect their product with good feelings in consumers' minds.

3. Many middle-aged Americans still associate the wee-oo sound of the theremin from the Beach Boys' Good Vibrations with images of beachgoers enjoying orange soft drinks.

4. The strategy of using hit songs in commercials can "backfire" when the listeners don't like the song or like it too much to think of it as an advertising "jingle."

5. Many aging baby boomers were disturbed to hear "Beatles" songs being used to sell shoes.

6. The rights to many Beatles songs, such as "Revolution", are no longer controlled by the Beatles.

7. Sometimes advertisements contain songs that seem to have no connection at all to the products being "plugged."

8. Many Iggy Pop fans wonder what on earth his song Lust for Life has to do with taking an expensive ocean cruise.

9. Not surprisingly, the song's more peculiar lyrics, including Well, that's like hypnotizing chickens, are omitted from the cruise-line advertisements.

10. Do consumers love the songs of their youth so much that merely "hearing" a song in an ad will make them buy that car?

52.1 Using parentheses and brackets

Revise the following sentences, using parentheses and brackets correctly. Change any other punctuation in the sentences as needed. (See *The Everyday Writer*, sections 52a–b.) Example:

Since the disputed presidential election of 2000, many observers (and not just from right-wing media outlets) have argued that U.S. journalists are not doing a thorough job of presenting political issues.

1. The words *media elite* have been said so often usually by people who are themselves elite members of the media that the phrase has taken on a life of its own.

Exercises 52.1 — Using parentheses and brackets

2. Are the media really elite, and are they really liberal, as talk-show regulars (Ann Coulter, for example argue)?

3. Media critic Eric Alterman has coined the term "so-called liberal media" [SCLM] because he believes that the media have been intimidated by criticism.

4. An article in the *Journal of Communication* discussing the outcome of recent U.S. elections explained that "claiming the media are liberally biased perhaps has become a core rhetorical strategy" used by conservatives, qtd. in Alterman 14.

5. Some progressive groups (including Fairness and Accuracy in Reporting (FAIR)) keep track of media coverage of political issues and campaigns.

6. However, liberals are not the only media watchdogs: right-wing organizations, including Accuracy in Media, (AIM) also closely examine the way political stories are reported.

7. The nonpartisan Campaign Desk website [sponsored by the *Columbia Journalism Review*] was dedicated to tracking media coverage of the 2004 presidential election.

8. According to the site's home page, the purpose of Campaign Desk was "to strengthen and deepen campaign coverage" as a resource for voters (most of whom rely on media coverage to make decisions about the candidates.)

9. Is truly objective coverage of hot-button issues and political candidates, (whether Republicans or Democrats,) ever possible?

10. And can we forget that as media consumers, we have an obligation to be an informed electorate (even though it's easy to pay attention only to the news that reinforces our own beliefs.)?

52.2 Using dashes

Revise the following sentences so that dashes are used correctly. If the sentence is correct as written, write C. (See *The Everyday Writer*, section 52c.) Example:

> In some states ^California, for example^ banks are no longer allowed to charge ATM users an additional fee for withdrawing money.

1. Many consumers accept the fact that they have to pay additional fees for services like bank machines if they don't want to pay, they don't have to use the service.

2. Nevertheless,—extra charges seem to be added to more and more services all the time.

3. Some of the charges are ridiculous why should hotels charge guests a fee for making a toll-free telephone call?

4. The hidden costs of service fees are irritating people feel that their bank accounts are being nibbled to death.

5. But some of the fees consumers are asked to pay—are more than simply irritating.

6. The "convenience charges"—that people have to pay when buying show tickets by telephone—are often a substantial percentage of the cost of the ticket.

7. If ticket buyers don't want to pay these "convenience charges" and who does? they must buy their tickets at the box office.

8. Finally, there are government fees that telephone companies and other large corporations are required to pay.

9. Telephone companies routinely pass these fees used to ensure Internet access to remote areas and schools along to their customers, implying that the government expects consumers to pay.

10. Many consumers are not aware that the government requires the corporations — not the general public — to pay these fees.

52.3 Using colons

Insert a colon in each of the following sentences that requires one. Remove any misused colons. Some sentences do not require a colon; if the sentence is correct as written, write C. (See *The Everyday Writer*, section 52d.) Example:

> Some fans of the *Star Wars* films have created a new online version of *Episode I: The Phantom Menace* that deletes all the scenes with Jar Jar Binks.

1. I was hoping to find a college with a male-female ratio of 1-2.

2. One of the most widely quoted passages in the Bible is from John 3, 16.

3. I like the music of: Red Hot Chili Peppers, Nine Inch Nails, and Radiohead.

4. Chopin, Kate. *The Awakening*. New York, Bantam Books, 1981.

5. He has traveled to many far-off, exotic destinations, including Tanzania, Nepal, and the Fijian Islands.

6. She was looking for all the most valuable qualities in a mate: kindness, honesty, generosity, and a good sense of humor.

7. Our guests enjoyed the meal, but as we left the restaurant I couldn't help whispering to my husband "We paid $75 for burgers and sodas?"

8. His list for Santa was sweet and simple, a new baseball glove, a book on dinosaurs, and a baby doll for his little sister, May.

9. My favorite Italian dishes include: eggplant parmesan, lasagna, and spaghetti and meatballs.

10. He wore the uniform of disaffected suburban youth, oversized clothing, slightly askew baseball hat, and multiple body piercings.

52.4 Using ellipses

Read the following passage. Then assume that the underlined portions have been left out in a reprinting of the passage. Indicate how you would use ellipses to indicate those deletions. (See *The Everyday Writer*, section 52f.) Example:

Saving money is difficult for young people in entry-level positions, but it is important.

Should young people who are just getting started in their careers think about saving for retirement? Those who begin to save in their twenties are making a wise financial decision. They are putting away money that can earn compound interest for decades. Even if they save only a hundred dollars a month, and even if they stop saving when they hit age thirty-five, the total forty years later will be impressive. On the other hand, people who wait until they are fifty to begin saving will have far less money put aside at the age of sixty-five. People who wait too long may face an impoverished retirement unless they are able to save thousands of dollars each month. Of course, no one knows how long he or she will live, but saving is a way of gambling on reaching retirement. Difficult as it may be to think about being sixty-five or seventy years old, young people should plan ahead.

52.5 Reviewing punctuation marks

Correct the punctuation in the following sentences. If the punctuation is already correct, write C. (See *The Everyday Writer,* Chapters 47–52.) Example:

> Children/ who are too young to speak/ are often frustrated because they cannot communicate their wishes.

1. Many American parents are willing to try almost anything prenatal music, infant flash cards, you name it to help their children succeed.

2. Some parental efforts do help children, for instance, children whose parents read to them are more likely to enjoy books.

3. Other schemes to make babies smarter, such as the so-called "Mozart effect," apparently don't make much difference.

4. A new idea that is "popular" with many parents of young children is sign language.

5. Researcher Joseph Garcia an expert in child development and in American Sign Language noticed that hearing babies with deaf parents often learned sign language before they could speak.

6. By sixteen to eighteen months, most children are able to speak simple words, and make themselves understood.

7. However, babies can communicate simple ideas to their parents starting at about eight months, if the infants learn signs

8. Garcia showed that parents could easily teach their children signs for words like please, more, sleepy, and hungry.

9. Garcia wrote a book called "Sign with Your Baby."

Reviewing punctuation marks 52.5 Exercises

10. Not surprisingly, parents bought the book, (and then the video,) and now sign-language classes for small children are easy to find.

11. Parents who go to signing classes with their infants and toddlers hope for a good outcome; better communication between parent and child and less frustration for both.

12. A study by California researchers found that seven-year-olds earned slightly higher IQ scores if they had learned to sign as infants.

13. It's not surprising that this studys results fueled the demand for more toddler sign-language classes.

14. The researchers who developed the study said that the best reason for parents to sign with their children was to allow the children "to communicate what they need and see".

15. One researcher, Dr Elizabeth Bates, told the "New York Times" that the hand movements that small children can learn are really gestures, not proper sign language.

16. Others contend that the childrens' hand movements stand for concepts so the movements are sign language.

17. Some parents fear that a child who learns to communicate by signs will have little incentive to speak researchers have found no evidence of this effect.

18. In fact children who can use sign language are often especially eager to learn how to speak.

19. While signing appears to have some benefits for the children who learn it not everyone feels that parents need to rush out to attend a class.

20. Any activity that gets parents to spend more time communicating with their children probably has it's benefits.

53.1 Capitalizing

Capitalize words as needed in each of the following sentences. (See *The Everyday Writer*, Chapter 53.) Example:

> T S E   T W   L   F
> *t. s. eliot*, who wrote *the waste land*, was an editor at *f*aber
>   F
> and *f*aber.

1. johnny depp appeared to be having a wonderful time playing captain jack sparrow in *pirates of the caribbean: the curse of the black pearl*.

2. the battle of lexington and concord was fought in april 1775.

3. i will cite the novels of vladimir nabokov, in particular *pnin* and *lolita*.

4. accepting an award for his score for the film *the high and the mighty*, dmitri tiomkin thanked beethoven, brahms, wagner, and strauss.

5. i wondered if my new levi's were faded enough.

6. We drove east over the hudson river on the tappan zee bridge.

7. senator trent lott was widely criticized after appearing to praise senator strom thurmond's segregationist past.

8. "bloody sunday" was a massacre of catholic protesters in derry, northern ireland, on january 30, 1972.

9. we had a choice of fast-food, chinese, or italian restaurants.

10. the town in the American south where i was raised had a statue of a civil war soldier in the center of main street.

54.1 Using abbreviations

Revise each of the following sentences to eliminate any abbreviations that would be inappropriate in academic writing. If a sentence is correct, write C. (See *The Everyday Writer*, sections 54a–g.) Example:

54.1 Using abbreviations — Exercises

        international
The ~~intl.~~ sport of belt sander racing began in a hardware store.

1. Nielson Hardware in Point Roberts, WA, was the site of the world's first belt sander race in 1989.

2. The power tools, ordinarily used for sanding wood, are placed on a thirty-ft. track and plugged in; the sander to reach the end first wins.

3. Today, the International Belt Sander Drag Race Association (IBSDRA) sponsors tours of winning sanders, an international championship, and a website that sells IBSDRA T-shirts.

4. There are three divisions of belt sander races: the stock div., which races sanders right out of the box; the modified div., which allows any motor the owner wants to add; and the decorative div., which provides a creative outlet for sander owners.

5. An average race lasts two seconds, but the world champion modified sander raced the track in 1.52 secs.

6. The fastest sanders run on very coarse sandpaper—a no. sixteen grit is an excellent choice if it's available.

7. Stock sanders are usually widely available brands, e.g., Mikita or Bosch.

8. The S-B Power Tool Co. in Chicago, maker of Bosch sanders, allows participants to race its tools, but the co. does not underwrite races.

9. Another tool company, the Do It Best Corp. of Wayne, Ind., sponsors races across the U.S. and Canada.

10. No one knows what % of the nation's power tools have been used for this kind of entertainment.

Exercises 54.2 Spelling out numbers and using figures

54.2 Spelling out numbers and using figures

Revise the numbers in the following sentences as necessary for correctness and consistency. If a sentence is correct, write C. (See *The Everyday Writer*, sections 54h–j.) Example:

>   seventh   one
> No correct answer choice was given for the ~~7th~~ question in part ~~1~~ of
> the test.

1. In the 35-to-44 age group, the risk is estimated to be about 1 in 2,500.
2. You could travel around the city for only 65 cents.
3. The amulet measured one and one-eighth by two and two-fifths inches.
4. Walker signed a three-year, $4.5 million contract.
5. The morning of September eleven, 2001, was cool and clear in New York City.
6. The parents considered twenty-five cents enough of an allowance for a five-year-old.
7. I drank 8 glasses of water, as the doctor had said, but then I had to get up 3 times during the night.
8. 307 miles long and 82 miles wide, the island offered little of interest.
9. Cable TV is now available to seventy-two percent of the population.
10. The department received 1,633 calls and forty-three letters.

55.1 Using Italics

In each of the following sentences, underline any words that should be italicized, and circle any italicized words that should not be. If a title requires quotation marks instead of italicization, add them. (See *The Everyday Writer*, Chapter 55.) Example:

The United States still abounds with regional speech—for example, many people in the Appalachians still use local words such as *crick* and *holler*.

1. *Regionalism*, a nineteenth-century literary movement, focused on the language and customs of people in areas of the country not yet affected by industrialization.

2. Regional writers produced some American classics, such as Mark Twain's Huckleberry Finn and James Fenimore Cooper's Last of the Mohicans.

3. Twain, not an admirer of Cooper's work, wrote a scathing essay about his predecessor called *The Literary Offenses of James Fenimore Cooper*.

4. Some of the most prolific regional writers were women like Kate Chopin, who wrote her first collection of short stories, Bayou Folk, to help support her family.

5. The stories in *Bayou Folk,* such as the famous *Désirée's Baby,* focus on the natives of rural Louisiana.

6. Chopin also departed from regional works to explore women's experiences of marriage, as in her short piece *The Story of an Hour.*

7. In Maine, Sarah Orne Jewett wrote sketches of rural life that appeared in the Atlantic Monthly.

8. She later turned these into a novel, Deephaven, which she hoped would "teach the world that country people were not . . . ignorant."

9. Her finest short story, *A White Heron,* and her celebrated novel *The Country of the Pointed Firs* also benefit from settings in Maine.

10. Many regional stories—Stephen Crane's *The Bride Comes to Yellow Sky* is a prime example—show the writer's concern that an isolated culture is in danger of disappearing.

Exercises

56.1 Using hyphens in compounds and with prefixes

Insert hyphens as needed. A dictionary will help you with some items. If an item does not require a hyphen, write C. (See *The Everyday Writer*, Chapter 56.) Example:

full-bodied wine

1. a thirty nine year old woman

2. my ex mother in law

3. singer songwriter Leslie Feist

4. devil may care attitude

5. mass produced goods

6. widely known poet

7. self righteous know it all

8. pro NAFTA crowd

9. ill gotten gains

10. one hundred and one Dalmatians

56.2 Using hyphens appropriately

Insert or delete hyphens as necessary in the following sentences. Use your dictionary if necessary. If a sentence is correct as printed, write C. (See *The Everyday Writer*, Chapter 56.) Example:

The bleary-eyed student finally stopped fighting sleep and went to bed.

1. His write-up on the race captured the excitement perfectly.

2. The House Unamerican Activities Committee was formed in 1937.

Using hyphens appropriately 56.2 Exercises

3. Joe seemed like a very angry-young-man.
4. Remember to drop-off your medical forms.
5. Her vacation was much-needed.
6. Please remind Jane to pick-up the clothes from the dry cleaners.
7. It's hard to believe that 90 percent of the world's water is salty.
8. I have a nine-year-old daughter, and the younger one is nearly five-years-old.
9. My mother is an ex-smoker; she quit when the warning appeared on all packs of cigarettes.
10. The sign up sheet is outside the gymnasium.

Glossary of Usage

GU-1 Selecting the appropriate word

Choose the appropriate word for each of the following sentences from the pair of words in parentheses. (See *The Everyday Writer*, Glossary of Usage.) Example:

She looked fragile and (<u>weak</u>/week).

1. The (explicit/implicit) perfume advertisement shocked readers.

2. I am too tired to walk any (farther/further).

3. I was (disinterested/uninterested) in hearing his latest excuse.

4. There are (fewer/less) graduates interested in education (than/then) there used to be.

5. School will be canceled today (due to/because of) inclement weather.

6. I will tell you the story, but please be (discreet/discrete).

7. One (affect/effect) of her stroke was impaired mobility.

8. I was reluctant to (loan/lend) him any more money.

9. We added insulation to the windows to (assure/ensure) that we would not have any drafts.

10. Jill felt (bad/badly) that Jack broke his crown.

11. If only we (could of/could have) stopped him from making that terrible mistake!

12. (Can/May) I have the next dance?

13. The students fully expected to be (censored/censured) by the headmaster for their inappropriate behavior.
14. That (continual/continuous) dripping from the faucet is driving me mad!
15. After (awhile/a while), we forgot the reason we had argued in the first place.
16. My English paper compares the works of Jane Austen (with/to) Charlotte Brontë's.
17. I used to support that candidate, but I cannot stand him (anymore/any more).
18. The way she (flouts/flaunts) her newfound wealth is appalling.
19. Her grades were among the most (distinct/distinctive) in the entire school.
20. She couldn't decide (whether or not/if) she should transfer to a different college.

GU-2 Editing inappropriate words

In each of the following sentences, remove or replace inappropriate words. If all the words in a sentence are appropriate, mark the sentence C. (See *The Everyday Writer,* Glossary of Usage.) Example:

          can
The pilot c̶a̶n̶'̶t̶ hardly see in such a fog.

1. I was good and ready for the final exam.
2. When he finally mastered the program, the trainee had a tendency to flaunt his newly acquired talent.
3. When I loose weight, my clothes become loose.
4. Johanna hanged the sheets on the line because the fresh air made them smell good, but the neighbors complained.

Exercises GU-2 *Editing inappropriate words*

5. Every time I go to the supermarket, I get less items for the same amount of money.

6. The supervisor and the trainee speak to each other everyday.

7. The principal could of been more encouraging when talking to the parents.

8. After gathering the chemicals and the instruments, you can proceed with the experiment.

9. Howie tried working out on a stationery bicycle, but he hated pedaling fast and going nowhere.

10. A small percent of the graduates weren't qualified for the entry-level positions.

11. If they are holding out for a consensus of opinion, they are going to have a long wait.

12. Swiss cheese is different than Jarlsberg.

13. The rich cream complements the figs.

14. Maybe we will fly to California to see Uncle Doug in the fall, but we may be too deeply in debt to take a vacation then.

15. Miranda has been working eleven-hour days since she learned that management is planning another round of layoffs.

16. She emigrated to New York in the 1920s.

17. Jackson Pollock created a new affect by dribbling paint on the canvas.

18. My visiting relatives made theirselves look like tourists by wearing white sneakers and by staring at all the tall buildings.

19. She is literally dying to see that movie.

20. Hopefully, it won't rain during the company outing.

Answers to the Even-Numbered Exercises

WRITING PROCESSES

EXERCISE 1.1 The top twenty: A quick guide to troubleshooting your writing

Some sentences have errors that most people would solve the same way; some sentences contain errors that have various solutions. Students may wish to make changes in addition to the corrections noted.

2. [wrong word] Popular spring break **destinations** over the years have included Mexican resorts, Florida beaches, and Caribbean islands.

4. [incomplete or missing documentation] According to one source, students may go on an alternative spring break to improve their résumé or to take an affordable trip, but they end up having an important emotional experience and building lifelong memories **(Delgado)**.

6. [unnecessary shift in verb tense] According to Valeria Delgado, one student reluctantly volunteered at the Boys and Girls Club in Newark, New Jersey, over spring break in 2011 and **found** that he enjoyed it much more than he thought he would ("Because Partying Is Too Mainstream").

8. [unnecessary or missing capitalization] It is always delightful to walk through Central Park on a warm summer day. Sunbathers set up towels on the lawn. People gather for concerts at the bandshell, while joggers move in groups along the reservoir. But the park is also magnificent during the stark, solitary days of winter.

10. [faulty sentence structure] The city of New York is made up of five boroughs—the Bronx, Manhattan, Queens, Brooklyn, and Staten

Island—and **comprises** an area of 322 square miles. It has more than 8 million residents, which makes New York the largest city in the United States.

12. [missing comma in a compound sentence] The annual tree-lighting ceremony at Rockefeller Center unofficially marks the beginning of the holiday season in the Big Apple. Statues of silvery horn-blowing angels encircle the plaza leading to the tree, and ice-skaters traverse the rink below. Taking center stage is the glorious tree itself, which twinkles with the glow of thousands of tiny lights. It is a magical time in the city for young and old alike.

14. [fused sentence] The Harlem Renaissance took place during the thirties **when** the upper Manhattan neighborhood became a focal point for African American artists, intellectuals, writers, and musicians. Some of the key figures of the period are Zora Neale Hurston, Langston Hughes, and Jean Toomer.

16. [poorly integrated quotation] Even John F. Kennedy was a fan of one local New York newspaper. **He once remarked:** "I don't think the intelligence reports are all that hot. Some days I get more out of the *New York Times.*"

18. [unnecessary comma] Many New Yorkers feel that Times Square has become too commercialized in recent years. The old character of the area is lost as big chain stores and restaurants populate the streets. Others argue that change is inevitable and that the new places bring money and jobs into the area.

20. [vague pronoun reference] The new law makes it illegal for drivers to talk on handheld cell phones, **and** many people are thrilled about it. Unfortunately, it is obvious that many motorists are choosing to ignore this piece of legislation.

CRITICAL THINKING AND ARGUMENT

EXERCISE 10.2 Recognizing fallacies
SUGGESTED ANSWERS

2. *In-crowd appeal:* This argument suggests to readers that they can be part of the financially successful crowd if they visit a particular website.

4. *Bandwagon appeal:* This passage uses "peer pressure" to convince the reader to watch the new television show.

6. *Flattery:* This argument tries to persuade the reader that because he or she is sensible about savings, he or she should invest in gold.

8. *Oversimplification:* It is a vast oversimplification to claim that legalizing marijuana would completely eradicate drug problems in this country.

10. *Either-or fallacy:* The writer suggests that *if* the school budget does not pass, the district's exam results will *necessarily* be disastrous, as if there is no other possible outcome in this scenario.

EXERCISE 11.1 Recognizing arguable statements

2. factual
4. factual
6. arguable
8. factual
10. arguable

EXERCISE 11.2 Demonstrating fairness
SUGGESTED ANSWERS

2. The writers demonstrate fairness by explaining that the volunteer depicted in the advertisement gives just a few hours of her day to support youth literacy, which makes the volunteer time commitment reasonable for most people. The writers also point out that Ruth Rusie's efforts are improving the education, income, and health of her community.

LANGUAGE

EXERCISE 27.1 Identifying stereotypes

2. Assumes that *all* women enjoy a particular kind of literature (and that no men do).
4. Implies that a chiropractor is not a legitimate medical practitioner.
6. Suggests that offensive and inappropriate behavior is somehow excusable because of gender predisposition to act a certain way.
8. Assumes that third graders could be attentive, focused, and calm only with the help of pharmaceuticals.

EXERCISE 27.3 Rewriting to eliminate offensive references
SUGGESTED ANSWERS

2. All the children in the kindergarten class will ask someone at home to help make cookies for the bake sale.
4. Acting as a spokesperson, Cynthia McDowell vowed that all elementary school teachers in the district would take their turns on the picket line until the school board agreed to resume negotiations.
6. Violinist Josh Mickle, last night's featured soloist, brought the crowd to its feet. (Or accept any version that omits mention of age and religion—both irrelevant here.)
8. The interdenominational service was attended by people of Jewish, Christian, Buddhist, and Islamic faiths.
10. Attorney Margaret Samuelson won her sixteenth case in a row last week.

EXERCISE 29.1 Using appropriate formality
SUGGESTED ANSWERS

2. I agree with many of his environmental policies, but that proposal is absolutely absurd.

4. We decided not to buy a bigger car that got terrible gas mileage and instead to keep our old Honda.

6. After she had raced to the post office at ten minutes to five, she realized that she had completely forgotten the fact that it was a federal holiday.

8. Moby Dick's enormous size was matched only by Ahab's obsessive desire to destroy him.

10. The class misbehaved so dreadfully in their regular teacher's absence that the substitute lost his temper.

EXERCISE 29.2 Determining levels of language
SUGGESTED ANSWERS

2. formal; *audience:* a prospective employer you want to impress

4. formal; *audience:* an informed audience whom you hope to convince

EXERCISE 29.3 Checking for correct denotation

2. apex; Correct word: nadir [or "low point"]

4. effected; Correct word: affected

6. Correct

8. delusion; Correct word: illusion

10. Retrofitting; Correct word: Reintroducing

EXERCISE 29.4 Revising sentences to change connotations

2. waltz away/little people who keep the company running/peanuts
Rewrite: CEOs are highly compensated with salary, stock options, and pension funds, while employees get comparatively little.

4. Tree huggers/ranted
Rewrite: Environmentalists protested the Explorer's gas mileage outside the Ford dealership.

6. Naive/stumble/blithely yank
   Rewrite: Often voters not familiar with using a voting machine will simply pull the handle without making informed choices.

8. mob/yelling/jabbing
   Rewrite: A large group of chanting, sign-waving protesters appeared.

EXERCISE 29.5 Considering connotation
SUGGESTED ANSWERS

2. *girl:* young lady, miss

4. *abide:* tolerate; *turns:* changes; *vital:* alive; *hold still:* contain their energy

EXERCISE 29.6 Using specific and concrete words
SUGGESTED ANSWERS

2. She could barely contain her unbridled excitement at the thought of beginning her new career. Good-bye to the old — to the squalid, windowless office and her lifeless co-workers. Good-bye to the myriad thankless tasks and the air of defeat that sucked the life out of all who entered the gloomy building. She was finally about to reap the rewards of all her hard work and sacrifice. Her new life beckoned.

4. The Smollings's children rarely get invited to other people's homes because they squabble constantly, demand endless adult attention, break dishes, and jump on furniture.

6. They started the backpacking trip in Barcelona, where they found a clean but lively hostel just off Las Ramblas. As soon as they entered the main courtyard area, they met travelers from Australia, Canada, and Ireland and made plans to catch the street fairs in Madrid the following week.

8. The feast at Mom's on Sunday was delicious as usual: roast chicken, garlic and sage stuffing, sweet garden peas, gallons of gravy, and half a fresh-baked apple pie each.

10. As the lights in the massive stadium dimmed, he felt his pulse quicken — then the thunderous roar of thousands of voices as the

shadowy figures appeared onstage and the first rich chords of the instruments were struck. He was transported instantly back in time, remembering the ecstatic joy of the very first concert he ever attended.

EXERCISE 29.7 Thinking about similes and metaphors

SUGGESTED ANSWERS

2. *great mounds of marshmallow fluff* (metaphor): clarifies the white and fluffy appearance of the clouds

4. *as if someone had punched him in the stomach* (simile): compares an emotion with a physical feeling

6. *like a magnolia corsage* (simile): makes vivid and concrete Mom Willie's heritage and suggests how positively she values it—and how proudly she "displays" it

8. *deep and soft like water moving in a cavern* (simile): compares the sound of her voice to water in a cavern, helping the reader to imagine the sound

10. *lounging* (metaphor): compares the horse in pasture to people relaxing; *cuddling up* (metaphor): emphasizes the pleasure the writer has reading mysteries; *top priority* (metaphor): reading as an activity of official importance

EXERCISE 29.8 Recognizing correct spellings

2. sites
4. friends; surprised
6. truly; lose
8. which; accepted
10. a lot; necessarily

EXERCISE 29.11 Spelling plurals

2. curricula
4. wolves
6. men-of-war
8. spies
10. boxes
12. mothers-in-law

STYLE

EXERCISE 30.2 Writing sentences with subordination
SUGGESTED ANSWERS

2. Although they had planned to go to Paris in the spring, they were forced to change their plans when their eldest child became ill.

4. Even though it was gray and rainy, we enjoyed driving along the scenic Pacific Coast Highway until it became too overcast to see anything.

EXERCISE 30.4 Emphasizing main ideas
SUGGESTED ANSWERS

2. The blogger known only as Atrios writes political commentary successfully enough to attract loyal readers, plenty of advertisers, and at least one lawsuit.

4. Coast Guard personnel conduct boating safety classes, monitor emergency radio channels, and sometimes must risk their own lives to save others.

6. Even though most people agree that recycling is generally beneficial, large numbers of people don't bother with recycling because it takes up time, uses up storage space, and can lead to unpleasant odors.

8. Although industrial dairy farmers insist that bovine growth hormone is harmless, the public wonders whether it could have strange effects on the human endocrine system, lead to digestive trouble, or cause cancer.

10. This all-in-one plant food I bought kept the bugs away, prevented fungus from forming, and led to the largest tomato crop I have ever seen.

EXERCISE 31.1 Matching subjects and predicates
SUGGESTED ANSWERS

2. In her books, many of which deal with the aftermath of slavery, are strong women characters.

   Her books, many of which deal with the aftermath of slavery, often feature strong women characters.

4. Although Morrison's depictions of African American families and neighborhoods are realistic, they also include supernatural elements.

   Morrison's depictions of African American families and neighborhoods are realistic, but they also include supernatural elements.

6. *Song of Solomon* was hailed as a masterpiece, winning the National Book Critics Circle Award in 1978.

   Song of Solomon, hailed as a masterpiece, won the National Book Critics Circle Award in 1978.

8. The title character in *Beloved* is the ghost of a murdered infant inhabiting the body of a young woman.

   Beloved features the ghost of a murdered infant inhabiting the body of a young woman.

10. In 1993, Toni Morrison became the first African American woman to be awarded the Nobel Prize in Literature.

    Toni Morrison, who was awarded the Nobel Prize in Literature in 1993, was the first African American woman to win that prize.

EXERCISE 31.2 Making comparisons complete, consistent, and clear

SUGGESTED ANSWERS

2. As the counselor pointed out, some jobs require more education than other jobs do.
4. Heart disease kills more people than cancer does.
6. Is the U.S. national debt higher than the debt of other countries?
8. Argentina and Peru were colonized by Spain, and Brazil was colonized by Portugal.
10. I enjoyed the movie more than John did.

EXERCISE 32.1 Creating parallel words or phrases

SUGGESTED ANSWERS

2. This summer, I want to learn to knit, to visit my grandparents, and to earn money for college.

4. In preparation for his wedding day, the groom rented a tux, chose his best man, and hired a band.//
6. When he got his promotion, he told the neighbors, called his family, and took out an ad in the newspaper.
8. The college athlete realized she would need to both practice longer and study harder.
10. Just as the demand for qualified teachers has increased, so has the supply dwindled.

EXERCISE 32.2 Revising sentences for parallelism
SUGGESTED ANSWERS

2. Many people in this country remember dancing to the mambo music of the 1950s and listening to that era's Latin bands.
4. Growing up near Havana and studying classical piano, Pérez Prado loved Cuban music.
6. Playing piano in Havana nightclubs, arranging music for a Latin big band, and joining jam sessions with the band's guitarists gave him the idea for a new kind of music.
8. Prado conducted his orchestra by waving his hands, moving his head and shoulders, and kicking his feet high in the air.
10. Pérez Prado, an innovator and a great musician, died in 1989.

EXERCISE 33.1 Revising for verb tense and mood
SUGGESTED ANSWERS

2. Correct
4. All health care workers should know that they have to keep their hands clean.
6. Hand washing can be repetitive, time consuming, and boring, but it is crucial to patient safety in every hospital.

Answers to the even-numbered exercises **33.4** Answers 147

8. The bacteria that cause these infections cannot travel through the air. They require physical contact to move from place to place.

10. Wash your hands frequently, and follow these instructions even if your skin gets dry.

EXERCISE 33.2 Eliminating shifts in voice and point of view

SUGGESTED ANSWERS

2. The police sent protesters to a distant "free speech zone" but allowed supporters to stand along the motorcade route.

4. Sea anemones thrive in coastal tide pools, but *they* cannot survive outside the water for very long.

6. If you have been pleased with a purchase on our site, would you consider reviewing it?

8. Do-it-yourselfers complete many home-improvement projects, but some people prefer to hire contractors.

10. The slow food movement emerged in France several decades ago; it set out to oppose the spread of fast-food chains in Europe.

EXERCISE 33.3 Eliminating shifts between direct and indirect discourse

SUGGESTED ANSWERS

2. She said that during a semester abroad, *she really missed all her friends.*

4. Loren Eiseley feels an urge to join the birds in their soundless flight, but in the end he knows that he cannot *and that he is only a man.*

EXERCISE 33.4 Eliminating shifts in tone and word choice

SUGGESTED ANSWERS

2. The Chinese invented noodles, even though many people think that the Italians created them.

4. The Guggenheim exhibit of African works of art, often misunderstood and undervalued by Western art historians, is a mind-expanding show.

EXERCISE 34.1 Eliminating unnecessary words and phrases
SUGGESTED ANSWERS

2. Shortly after Houdini's birth, his family moved to Appleton, where his father served as the only rabbi.

4. His many escapes included getting out of a giant sealed envelope without tearing it and walking out of jail cells that were said to be escape proof.

6. Clearly, Houdini did not want anyone to know his secrets.

8. Houdini's tremendous control over almost every muscle allowed him to contort his body into seemingly impossible positions.

10. On his deathbed, Houdini promised his wife that he would try to make contact with her from beyond the grave, but so far, he has never been able to get in touch.

SENTENCE GRAMMAR

EXERCISE 36.1 Identifying verbs and verb phrases

2. Holi <u>is known</u> as the festival of colors, not only because spring <u>brings</u> flowers but also because Holi celebrations always <u>include</u> brightly colored dyes.

4. During Holi, people <u>toss</u> fistfuls of powdered dyes or dye-filled water balloons at each other and <u>sing</u> traditional Holi songs.

6. Any person who <u>is walking</u> outside during a Holi celebration <u>will</u> soon <u>be wearing</u> colored powders or colored water.

8. Some people <u>wear</u> white clothing for Holi.

10. <u>Doesn't</u> Holi <u>sound</u> like fun?

EXERCISE 36.2 Identifying nouns and articles

Nouns are set in *italics;* articles are set in **boldface.**

2. *Slavery;* **the;** *colonization; America*
4. *broccoli; asparagus*
6. *Doctors; autism*
8. *Nightlife; Georgetown;* **the;** *sun*
10. *Journalists; sources;* **a;** *case; security*

EXERCISE 36.3 Identifying pronouns and antecedents

Pronouns are set in *italics;* antecedents are set in **boldface.**

2. **dogs;** *that; their*
4. *they; their;* **volunteers; puppy;** *its*
6. *you;* **puppy;** *its;* **coat;** *that; it*
8. *Some;* **pups;** *these*
10. *you; your*

EXERCISE 36.4 Identifying adjectives and adverbs

Adjectives are set in *italics;* adverbs are set in **boldface.**

2. **seriously; how; well;** *their; intense; public*
4. *The; that; lovely;* **uncomfortably;** *narrow;* **much; too;** *expensive*
6. **not;** *the; smallest; quietest; the*
8. *The;* **most;** *instructive; the;* **unfortunately;** *the; longest*
10. *Imminent; many;* **constantly**

EXERCISE 36.5 Adding adjectives and adverbs

SUGGESTED ANSWERS

2. Surely, most of us enjoy classic movies.

4. A multinational corporation can fire undependable workers.
6. The unpopulated boardwalk crosses the bleak, wintry beach.
8. The mainstream media are determinedly ignoring his candidacy.
10. Which way did you say the hunted pair went yesterday?

EXERCISE 36.6 Identifying prepositions

2. upon; into; as
4. Due to; of; through; with
6. In spite of; from
8. with; above; of; beyond
10. From; upon; in; of

EXERCISE 36.7 Identifying conjunctions

2. not only . . . but also [two parts of a correlative conjunction]; and
4. When
6. Although; and; as though
8. whether . . . or [two parts of a correlative conjunction]; after
10. because

EXERCISE 36.8 Identifying conjunctions and interjections

2. Although (SUBORD)
4. after (SUBORD); Ouch (interjection)
6. Until (SUBORD)
8. Aha (interjection); but (COORD)
10. so (COORD)

EXERCISE 36.9 Identifying the parts of speech

2. is selling—verb; cosmetics—noun; attractive—adjective
4. Middle Earth—noun (proper); while—conjunction (subordinating); on—preposition
6. In—preposition; that—pronoun (relative); consistently—adverb; our—pronoun (possessive)
8. also—adverb; safety—noun; that—pronoun (relative)
10. hey—interjection; bought—verb; who—pronoun (relative); the—article (adjective)

EXERCISE 37.1 Identifying subjects and predicates

The subject is set in *italics*; the predicate is set in **boldface**.

2. *It* **was an immense crowd, two thousand at the least and growing every minute.**
4. **In a job like that,** *you* **see the dirty work of Empire at close quarters.**
6. *The hangman, a gray-haired convict in the white uniform of the prison,* **was waiting beside his machine.**
8. **Would** *I* **please come and do something about it?**
10. *We* **set out for the gallows.**

EXERCISE 37.2 Identifying subjects

Complete subjects are set in *italics*; simple subjects are set in **boldface**.

2. *Ancient Chinese, Greeks, and Romans, as well as South and Central Americans,* **all** played versions of "football."
4. In 1863, *eleven London soccer* **clubs** sent their representatives to the Freemason's Tavern for a meeting.
6. In the minority were *the* **proponents** *of rugby*, who were against rules that forbade ball carrying.

8. *The historical* **meeting** led to the eventual split between rugby and football and to the founding of the Football Association.

10. **It** is the most widely watched sporting event in the world.

EXERCISE 37.3 Identifying predicates

Predicates are set in *italics*.

2. *favored* [TV] *capital punishment* [DO]

4. *called* [TV] *capital punishment* [DO] *"cruel and unusual"* [OC] ... *outlawed* [TV] *it* [DO] *in 1972*

6. *was developed* [IV] *as an alternative to older execution methods such as hanging*

8. *has given* [TV] *more than a hundred prisoners on death row* [IO] *their freedom* [DO]

10. *were* [LV] *the only industrialized nations* [SC] ... *used* [TV] *the death penalty* [DO]

EXERCISE 37.4 Identifying prepositional phrases

2. from Italy; in an overcrowded boat; among his countrymen and women

4. Without any formal education; against all odds; in business

EXERCISE 37.5 Using prepositional phrases

SUGGESTED ANSWERS

2. Polytetrafluoroethylene (PTFE) is the chemical name for Teflon.

4. The substance allows food to cook in a pan without sticking.

6. Early nonstick cookware coating tended to peel off the surface of the pan at the slightest touch of a metal utensil.

8. The primer holds the PTFE coat in place with a physical bond, not a chemical one.

10. As an adjective, the word *Teflon* describes a person who seems to get out of sticky situations easily.

EXERCISE 37.6 Identifying verbal phrases

2. inf—*To check Turing's hypothesis;* inf—*to determine if any of them can successfully mimic a human conversation*
4. part—*Programmed for artificial intelligence;* inf—*to imitate humans in Internet chat rooms*
6. gerund, subject—*Teaching a machine artificial intelligence*
8. gerund, subject—*Receiving a $2,000 consolation prize*
10. gerund—*being a computer*

EXERCISE 37.7 Identifying prepositional, verbal, absolute, and appositive phrases

2. verbal—*outlined against the sky;* prep—*against the sky;* verbal—*to move*
4. absolute—*her fingers clutching the fence;* verbal—*clutching the fence*
6. verbal—*Floating on my back;* prep—*on my back*
8. app—*the leader of the group;* prep—*of the group;* verbal—*to relinquish any authority*
10. verbal—*Shocked into silence;* prep—*into silence;* verbal—*fixed on the odd creature;* prep—*on the odd creature*

EXERCISE 37.8 Adding prepositional, verbal, absolute, and appositive phrases

SUGGESTED ANSWERS

2. Teresa looked at her mother, her eyes searching for the familiar face that now seemed so old.
4. Having thoughtlessly locked ourselves out while the bathtub filled with water, we were uncertain what to do.
6. Gazing out the window, he wondered about the disappearance of the buffalo nickel, replaced by a smaller, less interesting five-cent coin.
8. Unopened, the letter lay on the desk in its gleaming white envelope looking very inviting.

10. Ten hours of sleep, almost twice her usual amount, exhausted her, leaving her head almost too heavy to lift from the pillow.

EXERCISE 37.9 Using verbal, absolute, and appositive phrases to combine sentences

SUGGESTED ANSWERS

2. If you plan to fly into Dublin, you can backpack your way around the country from there.

4. The Ballsbridge area, home to foreign embassies and many other sites, is another fine place to visit.

6. The Irish National Gallery, worth checking out for art lovers, is located at Merrion Square West.

8. Stand on the Martello Tower in Sandycove, the Irish Sea before you.

10. Saying good-bye to Dublin will be difficult, but there is much more of the country to explore.

EXERCISE 37.10 Identifying dependent clauses

Dependent clauses are set in *italics*.

2. *when spring arrives in the South*; sub conj—when

4. *Although the Appalachian mountain range has relatively low peaks*; sub conj—Although

6. *Because the Appalachian Trail lies mainly in wilderness*; sub conj—Because

8. *that have become accustomed to humans*; rel pron—that

10. *how to react to an aggressive bear to minimize the danger*; rel pron—how

EXERCISE 37.11 Adding dependent clauses

SUGGESTED ANSWERS

2. Everyone in a family that spends the day in separate places may have high expectations for time together.

4. Whining, which all children do from time to time, is difficult to listen to and easy to stop with a new toy or an extra video viewing.

6. Misbehaving children who expect to get their own way wear out their welcome quickly.

8. Parents who want to set a good example must learn to stick to their own rules.

10. Even if children protest against discipline, which everyone resists from time to time, they want to know how to behave.

EXERCISE 37.12 Distinguishing between phrases and clauses

Dependent clauses are set in *italics*; phrases are set in **boldface**.

2. **as beyond recall, beyond recall**—prep phrases
4. **of encountering a Perelman piece**—prep phrase; **encountering a Perelman piece**—verbal phrase; **in a magazine**—prep phrase
6. **at a glance**—prep phrase; *that Professor Strunk omitted needless words*
8. *When I start a book*; *what my characters are going to do*; **to do**—verbal; **for their eccentric behavior**—prep phrase
10. *When I wrote "Death of a Pig"*; **of a Pig**—prep phrase; **of what actually happened**—prep phrase; **on my place**—prep phrase; **to my pig**—prep phrase; *who died*; **to me**—prep phrase; *who tended him*; **in his last hours**—prep phrase

Imitation sentences will vary.

EXERCISE 37.13 Classifying sentences grammatically and functionally

2. complex, declarative
4. compound-complex, declarative
6. complex, declarative
8. compound, declarative
10. simple, exclamatory

EXERCISE 37.14 Expressing subjects and objects explicitly

SUGGESTED ANSWERS

2. Correct

4. There are problems with doing everything online, of course.

6. There are small-time thieves and juvenile pranksters disrupting online services.

8. A hacker can get enormous amounts of online data, even if they are supposed to be secure.

10. Internet users must use caution and common sense online, but it is also essential for online information to be safeguarded by security experts.

EXERCISE 37.15 Using noun clauses, infinitives, and gerunds appropriately

SUGGESTED ANSWERS

2. We discussed going to a movie, but we could not agree on what to see.

4. Correct

6. Her mother stopped driving on her ninetieth birthday.

8. Correct

10. We appreciated getting the invitation.

EXERCISE 37.16 Using adjective clauses appropriately

SUGGESTED ANSWERS

2. Some students who want to practice speaking more asked us all to help prepare a dinner.

4. A reporter attended the dinner and wrote an article in which he praised the chefs.

6. My mother makes many delicious dishes that come from our homeland.

8. We all come from different places, so those of us who were cooking together had to speak English to communicate.

10. Correct

EXERCISE 38.1 Using irregular verb forms

2. was; said; was
4. broke; lay
6. met; fell
8. kept; was
10. grown; spread

EXERCISE 38.2 Editing verb forms

2. have went—went
4. Correct
6. knew—known
8. swum—swam
10. lend—lent

EXERCISE 38.3 Distinguishing between *lie* and *lay*, *sit* and *set*, *rise* and *raise*

2. laid
4. Sit
6. lie
8. raise
10. rose

EXERCISE 38.4 Deciding on verb tenses

2. begin; dates
4. have opened
6. was looking; suggested
8. are searching; requires
10. will check; is teaching

EXERCISE 38.5 Sequencing tenses

2. Until I *started* knitting again last month, I *had forgotten* how.
4. After Darius said that he wanted to postpone college, I *tried* to talk him out of it.
6. I *had imagined* the job *would be finished* by that point.

8. When he *was* twenty-one, he *wanted to become* a millionaire by the age of thirty.

10. *Having worked* at the law firm for five years, she *was* ready for a change.

EXERCISE 38.6 Converting the voice of a sentence

Answers may vary slightly.

2. The hungry children *devoured* the mouthwatering butter cookies.

4. Jerry *ate* the last doughnut in the box just a few minutes ago.

6. For months, the mother kangaroo *protects, feeds,* and *teaches* its baby how to survive.

8. The first snow of winter *covered* the lawns and rooftops.

10. The store *was forced* to close because of a lack of customers.

EXERCISE 38.7 Using subjunctive mood

2. Correct

4. would have heard — had heard

6. knows — know

8. should not take — not take

10. was — were

EXERCISE 38.8 Writing conditional sentences

SUGGESTED ANSWERS

2. If the dot-com boom had continued, that prediction might have come true.

4. If any computer job is announced these days, hundreds of qualified people apply for it.

Answers to the even-numbered exercises **38.11** **Answers**

6. If Indian workers required as much money as Americans do to live, U.S. companies would not be as eager to outsource computer work to the other side of the world.

8. Would fewer Americans be unemployed right now if the dot-com boom had never happened?

10. If American students want to prepare for a secure future, they should consider a specialty like nursing, in which jobs are available and the work cannot be sent abroad.

EXERCISE 38.10 Using specified forms of verbs

SUGGESTED ANSWERS

2. The dogs at the kennel barked all night long.
   The dogs at the kennel were barking all night.

4. I brought a present to him on his birthday.
   I am bringing him a present on his birthday.

6. Those teenagers consumed three dozen hamburgers and two cases of pop.
   When I left the picnic, the teenagers were consuming the last of the carrot cake.

8. The pasta steamed in the buffet tray.
   The pasta is steaming up the kitchen.

10. This hamburger tastes good.
    The hamburger had tasted fine until I noticed the fly on the bun.

EXERCISE 38.11 Identifying tenses and forms of verbs

2. was walking: past progressive; struck: simple past

4. has admired: present perfect

6. have attempted: present perfect

8. has driven: present perfect
10. had forgotten: past perfect

EXERCISE 38.12 Using verbs appropriately

2. The Rosetta Stone is *covered* with inscriptions in three ancient languages.
4. At that time, scholars *had been* puzzled by hieroglyphics for centuries.
6. A scholar named Jean-François Champollion could *understand* both ancient Greek and modern Egyptian, known as Coptic.
8. From the Coptic inscription, he *learned* to read the hieroglyphics.
10. The hieroglyphics, Demotic, and Greek texts all *contain* a decree from an ancient king.

EXERCISE 39.2 Using determiners appropriately; using articles conventionally

2. Dangerous germs such as salmonella are commonly found in some foods.
4. Many people regularly clean their kitchen counters and cutting boards to remove bacteria.
6. Every time someone wipes a counter with a dirty sponge, more germs are spread around the kitchen.
8. According to research studies, young single men's kitchens tend to have fewer germs than many other kitchens.
10. To eliminate many dangerous bacteria from the kitchen, cooks should wash their hands frequently.

EXERCISE 40.1 Selecting verbs that agree with their subjects

2. are
4. have
6. is
8. was
10. has

EXERCISE 40.2 Making subjects and verbs agree

2. are—is
4. use—uses
6. sets—set
8. Correct
10. allows—allow
12. Correct
14. belongs—belong

EXERCISE 41.1 Using subjective case pronouns

2. they
4. they
6. they
8. We
10. they

EXERCISE 41.2 Using objective case pronouns

2. Correct
4. When we asked, the seller promised <u>us</u> that the software would work on our computer.
6. The teacher praised <u>them</u> for asking thoughtful questions.
8. Correct
10. I couldn't tell who was more to blame for the accident, <u>you</u> or Susan.

EXERCISE 41.3 Using possessive case pronouns

2. mine
4. Her
6. their
8. her
10. yours

EXERCISE 41.4 Using *who*, *whoever*, *whom*, or *whomever*

2. whoever
4. whoever
6. Whom
8. who
10. whoever

EXERCISE 41.5 Using pronouns in compound structures, appositives, elliptical clauses; choosing between *we* and *us* before a noun

2. he
4. him
6. her
8. them
10. he
12. us
14. I

EXERCISE 41.6 Maintaining pronoun-antecedent agreement

SUGGESTED ANSWERS

2. A child-free person may feel that people with children see his or her time as less valuable than their own.

4. Child-free employees may feel that they have to subsidize family medical plans at work for people who have children.

6. However, a community has to consider the welfare of its children because caring for and educating children eventually benefits everyone.

8. Almost no one would be able to afford to have children if parents were expected to pay for educating and training their offspring entirely without help.

10. As writer Barbara Kingsolver once pointed out, in their old age even people without children will probably need the services of a doctor or a mechanic.

EXERCISE 41.7 Clarifying pronoun reference

SUGGESTED ANSWERS

2. Not long after the company set up the subsidiary, the subsidiary went bankrupt.
   Not long after the company set up the subsidiary, the company went bankrupt.

4. When Deyon was reunited with his father, the boy wept.
   When Deyon was reunited with his father, his father wept.

6. The weather forecast said to expect snow in the overnight hours.

8. Lear divides his kingdom between the two older daughters, Goneril and Regan, whose extravagant professions of love are more flattering than the simple affection of the youngest daughter, Cordelia. The consequences of this error in judgment soon become apparent, as the older daughters prove neither grateful nor kind to him.

10. The visit to the pyramids was canceled because of the recent terrorist attacks on tourists there, so Kay, who had waited years to see the monuments, was disappointed.

EXERCISE 42.1 Using adjectives and adverbs appropriately

2. defiant — defiantly; modifies *crosses*

4. sadly — sad; modifies *you*

6. relievedly — relieved; modifies *you*

8. oddly — odd; modifies *"words"*

10. Lucky — Luckily; modifies *available*

EXERCISE 42.2 Using comparative and superlative modifiers appropriately

SUGGESTED ANSWERS

2. the famousest — the most famous

4. best—better

6. the worse—the worst

8. more—more than funny ones

10. littler—less

EXERCISE 42.3 Positioning modifiers

2. dusty, dry, uninhabited mining town

4. crowded local beach

6. coed volleyball team

8. worthwhile educational program

10. X-rated movie rental

EXERCISE 43.1 Revising sentences with misplaced modifiers

SUGGESTED ANSWERS

2. Singing with verve, the tenor captivated the entire audience.

4. The city spent approximately $12 million on the new stadium.

6. On the day in question, the patient was not able to breathe normally.

8. The clothes that I was giving away were full of holes.

10. A wailing baby with a soggy diaper was quickly kissed by the candidate.

EXERCISE 43.2 Revising squinting modifiers, disruptive modifiers, and split infinitives

SUGGESTED ANSWERS

2. He vividly remembered enjoying the sound of Mrs. McIntosh's singing.

4. The mayor promised that after her reelection she would not raise taxes.

   After her reelection, the mayor promised that she would not raise taxes.

6. The collector who originally owned the painting planned to leave it to a museum.

   The collector who owned the painting planned originally to leave it to a museum.

8. Doctors can now restore limbs that have been partially severed to a functioning condition.

   Doctors can now restore limbs that have been severed to a partially functioning condition.

10. The speaker said he would answer questions when he finished.

    When he finished, the speaker said he would answer questions.

12. After a long summer under the blazing sun, the compost smelled pretty bad when I turned it.

14. After a long day at work and an evening class, Stella did not want to argue about who was going to do the dishes.

    Stella did not want to argue about who was going to do the dishes after a long day at work and an evening class.

EXERCISE 43.3 Revising dangling modifiers

SUGGESTED ANSWERS

2. When interviewing grieving relatives, reporters show no consideration for their privacy.

4. Chosen for their looks, newscasters often have weak journalistic credentials.

6. Assuming that viewers care about no one except Americans, editorial boards for network news shows reject many international stories.

8. Horrified by stories of bloodshed, most viewers don't recognize the low probability of becoming the victim of crime or terrorism.

10. Not covering less sensational but more common dangers such as reckless driving and diabetes, news broadcasts do not tell viewers what is really likely to hurt them.

EXERCISE 44.1 Using prepositions idiomatically

2. into/from/in; during/in
4. up/down/on; on/onto
6. on
8. with
10. to

EXERCISE 44.2 Recognizing and using two-word verbs

2. two-word verb
4. two-word verb
6. verb + preposition
8. two-word verb
10. two-word verb

EXERCISE 45.1 Revising comma splices and fused sentences

Only one suggested answer is given for each numbered item.

2. The group Human Rights Watch filed a report on Mauritania, a nation in northwest Africa.
4. Members of Mauritania's ruling group are called the Beydanes, an Arab Berber tribe also known as the White Moors.
6. In modern-day Mauritania, many of the Haratin are still slaves; they serve the Beydanes.
8. Mauritania outlawed slavery in 1981, but little has been done to enforce the law.
10. Physical force is not usually used to enslave the Haratin. Rather, they are held by the force of conditioning.

12. By some estimates 300,000 former slaves, who are psychologically and economically dependent, still serve their old masters.

14. In addition, there may be as many as 90,000 Haratin still enslaved; some Beydanes have refused to free their slaves unless the government pays compensation.

16. Of course, slavery must have existed in Mauritania, or there would have been no compelling reason to make a decree to abolish it in 1981.

18. Both the slaveholding Beydanes and the enslaved Haratin are made up largely of Muslims, so some people in Mauritania see resistance to slavery in their country as anti-Muslim.

20. Islamic authorities in Mauritania have agreed that all Muslims are equal; therefore, one Muslim must not enslave another.

EXERCISE 46.1 Eliminating sentence fragments

SUGGESTED ANSWERS

2. September is the perfect time to run outdoors, thus avoiding the wait for a treadmill at a crowded gym.

4. For new college students who live on campus, the Columbus Day weekend often marks the first visit back home. For others, it is Thanksgiving. In any case, the event is often emotionally charged for both parents and students alike.

6. I can't tell if he is skipping the Halloween party because he is genuinely ill, or he just doesn't have an idea for a costume.

8. My sister and her husband are hosting Thanksgiving dinner at their house this year. With Christmas at my parents' house and New Year's Eve at my cousin's, it should be a busy holiday season!

10. Autumn often begins with hot, summerlike weather. It is sometimes warm enough to go swimming outdoors! And by the end of the season, people are shoveling out their driveways and replacing flip-flops with snow boots.

PUNCTUATION AND MECHANICS

EXERCISE 47.1   Using a comma to set off introductory elements

2. Unlike sterilization, pasteurization does not destroy all the pathogens in a food.

4. While there are many methods of pasteurization, the most commonly used is called HTST (for High Temperature/Short Time).

6. Concerned about the helpful bacteria killed in the pasteurization process, some people recommend drinking raw milk.

8. In stark contrast to their "mainstream" counterparts, cows on raw milk dairy farms are not fed commercial feed.

10. Whatever your opinion on this issue, it is unlikely that the debate will be settled soon.

EXERCISE 47.2   Using a comma in compound sentences
SUGGESTED ANSWERS

2. A biological virus cannot replicate itself, *so* it must inject its DNA into a cell in order to reproduce.

4. These viruses can be totally destructive or basically benign, *yet* when people think of computer viruses, they generally think of the former.

6. Viruses can be distributed through downloads, *or* they can be spread through black-market software.

8. Children love to download computer games from sites they might be unfamiliar with, *so* parents and teachers should teach children about computer security.

10. The world of computer viruses might seem daunting, *but* by following a few basic safety rules, computer users can largely protect themselves.

EXERCISE 47.3 Recognizing restrictive and nonrestrictive elements

2. The clause *that preserves a cadaver* is essential for the sentence to have any meaning at all. Therefore, it should not take commas.
4. Do not set off the phrase *standing in the hall outside the classroom*, or readers will not know which girl is meant.
6. The appositive phrase *reading web logs* is not needed to make the meaning of the sentence clear. It should be set off with commas.
8. The appositive that describes Karl Marx is providing additional but not essential information. Therefore, *an important nineteenth-century political philosopher* should be set off from the rest of the sentence.
10. The phrase *an ancient tribe* provides additional information and should be set off from the rest of the sentence with commas.
12. The participial phrase *made of wood* is restrictive because the meaning of the sentence is not complete without it. That the houses are made of wood is what often allows them to survive earthquakes. Therefore, the phrase should not take commas.
14. The clause *who rescued her puppy* is restrictive because only the man who rescued the puppy won the gratitude. The winning of eternal gratitude is restricted to the man who rescued the puppy. Therefore, the clause should not take commas.

EXERCISE 47.4 Using commas to set off items in a series

2. I am looking forward to turning eighteen, being able to vote, and perhaps serving in the military.
4. The moon circles the earth, the earth revolves around the sun, and the sun is just one star among many in the Milky Way galaxy.
6. He is a brilliant, demanding, renowned concert pianist.
8. My top three favorite nineties bands are Pearl Jam, Nirvana, and Soundgarden, in that order.
10. Superficial observation does not provide accurate insight into people's lives—how they feel, what they believe in, how they respond to others.

EXERCISE 47.5 Using commas to set off parenthetical and transitional expressions, contrasting elements, interjections, direct address, and tag questions

2. Doctor Ross, you are over an hour late for our appointment.
4. The West, in fact, has become solidly Republican in presidential elections.
6. Captain Kirk, I'm a doctor, not a madman.
8. One must consider the society as a whole, not just its parts.
10. Mary announced, "Kids, I want you to clean your rooms, not make a bigger mess."

EXERCISE 47.6 Using commas with dates, addresses, titles, numbers, and quotations

2. Correct
4. "Who can match the desperate humorlessness of the adolescent who thinks he is the first to discover seriousness?" asks P. J. Kavanaugh.
6. On July 21, 1969, Neil Armstrong became the first person to walk on the moon.
8. "Neat people are lazier and meaner than sloppy people," according to Suzanne Britt.
10. Correct

EXERCISE 47.7 Eliminating unnecessary commas

2. Insomniacs do indeed wake up at night, but studies have demonstrated that they also have trouble napping during the day.
4. In many cases, insomniacs suffer from anxiety.
6. Correct
8. Sleep therapists recommend going to bed at the same time every night, not watching television in bed, and not reading in bed.
10. While tired people are more dangerous drivers and less productive workers, no one knows for certain if insomnia can actually make them sick.

EXERCISE 48.1 Using semicolons to link independent clauses

2. Teenagers today don't spend all their time on the telephone; instead, they go online and send each other instant messages.
4. She was distressed about his failing grade in English; on the other hand, she was thrilled about his A in math.
6. Smith Street in Brooklyn is a popular area filled with restaurants and shops; many visitors to New York City now include it on their sightseeing itineraries.
8. Establishing your position in an office is an important task; your profile will mold your relationships with other staff members.
10. That resort is ideal for beginner skiers; in addition, it offers snowboarding classes.

EXERCISE 48.2 Revising misused semicolons

2. Verbal scores have decreased by more than fifty-four points, while math scores have decreased by more than thirty-six.
4. Finally, I found her at the Humane Society: a beautiful shepherd-collie mix who likes children and plays well with cats.
6. He enjoys commuting to work on the train, although it can get crowded at rush hour.
8. Correct
10. I will meet you at the movies as soon as I finish writing my term paper.

EXERCISE 49.1 Using periods appropriately

2. She has raised disturbing questions about why parents sometimes kill their offspring.
4. Human parents, even in recent centuries, may actively or passively have limited their children's chances to grow up.
6. The term "parent-offspring conflict" was coined by Robert Trivers, PhD.

8. Many mothers are indeed willing to put up with a great deal from their children, from 2:00 A.M. feedings through requests for college tuition.

10. Describing a mother's crime against her child as "inhuman" is neither accurate nor helpful in preventing future tragedies.

EXERCISE 49.2 Using question marks appropriately

2. "Which Harry Potter book did you like best?" Georgia asked Harriet.

4. "Who wants to go to the pool with me?" asked May.

6. Correct

8. We began to ask what might fix the problem—restarting the computer? closing other programs? using a different browser?

10. I asked her if she would be much longer in the bathroom.

EXERCISE 49.3 Using exclamation points appropriately

SUGGESTED ANSWERS

2. Oh no! We've lost the house!

4. "Go! Go! Go!" roared the crowd as the quarterback sped toward the end zone.

6. It was an ordinary school day, so the child once again came home to an empty house.

8. She exclaimed, "It's too hot!"

10. "This is ridiculous!" sputtered the diner as the waiter brought the wrong order again.

EXERCISE 50.1 Using apostrophes to signal possession

2. Recipients who pass on messages want everyone to hear about a *child's* inspiring fight against cancer or about some dangerous drug, product, or disease.

4. A *hoax's* creators count on *recipients'* kind hearts and concern for the well-being of their families and friends.

6. Have you heard the one about how *deodorants'* ingredients supposedly clog your pores and cause cancer?

8. Some of these scares are probably intended to damage certain *corporations'* reputations by spreading rumors about products.

10. The *Internet's* speed has made such anonymous rumors spread more rapidly than anyone would have thought possible twenty years ago.

EXERCISE 50.2 Using apostrophes to create contractions

2. I won't be able to go swimming this afternoon if it's pouring.

4. He's valedictorian for the class of 2008.

6. The clothes that I'm washing now didn't really get too dirty.

8. The distributor says that your order hasn't received its approval from the business office.

10. Isn't that the new jazz club that's open on weekends?

EXERCISE 51.1 Using quotation marks to signal direct quotations

2. Correct

4. To paraphrase his words, the planet is in deep trouble if we don't start reducing carbon emissions.

6. Correct

8. "I could not believe the condition of my hometown," he wrote.

10. "Is the computer plugged in?" the technical support operator asked, prompting Harry to snarl, "Yes, I'm not a complete idiot."

EXERCISE 51.2 Using quotation marks for titles and definitions

2. My dictionary defines *isolation* as "the quality or state of being alone."
4. Kowinski uses the term *mallaise* to mean "physical and psychological disturbances caused by mall contact."
6. "The little that is known about gorillas certainly makes you want to know more," writes Alan Moorehead in his essay "A Most Forgiving Ape."
8. If you had ever had "Stairway to Heaven" running through your head for four days straight, you would not like Led Zeppelin either.
10. Amy Lowell challenges social conformity in her poem "Patterns."

EXERCISE 51.3 Using quotation marks appropriately

SUGGESTED ANSWERS

2. Television commercials have frequently used popular songs as an effective way to connect their product with good feelings in consumers' minds.
4. The strategy of using hit songs in commercials can backfire when the listeners don't like the song or like it too much to think of it as an advertising jingle.
6. The rights to many Beatles songs, such as "Revolution," are no longer controlled by the Beatles.
8. Many Iggy Pop fans wonder what on earth his song "Lust for Life" has to do with taking an expensive ocean cruise.
10. Do consumers love the songs of their youth so much that merely hearing a song in an ad will make them buy that car?

EXERCISE 52.1 Using parentheses and brackets

2. Are the media really elite, and are they really liberal, as talk-show regulars (Ann Coulter, for example) argue?

Answers to the even-numbered exercises

4. An article in the *Journal of Communication* discussing the outcome of recent U.S. elections explained that "claiming the media are liberally biased perhaps has become a core rhetorical strategy" used by conservatives (qtd. in Alterman 14).

6. However, liberals are not the only media watchdogs: right-wing organizations, including Accuracy in Media (AIM), also closely examine the way political stories are reported.

8. According to the site's home page, the purpose of Campaign Desk was "to strengthen and deepen campaign coverage" as a resource for voters (most of whom rely on media coverage to make decisions about the candidates).

10. And can we forget that as media consumers, we have an obligation to be an informed electorate (even though it's easy to pay attention only to the news that reinforces our own beliefs)?

EXERCISE 52.2 Using dashes

2. Nevertheless, extra charges seem to be added to more and more services all the time.

4. The hidden costs of service fees are irritating—people feel that their bank accounts are being nibbled to death.

6. The "convenience charges" that people have to pay when buying show tickets by telephone are often a substantial percentage of the cost of the ticket.

8. Correct

10. Correct

EXERCISE 52.3 Using colons

2. One of the most widely quoted passages in the Bible is from John 3:16.

4. Chopin, Kate. *The Awakening*. New York: Bantam Books, 1981.

6. Correct

8. His list for Santa was sweet and simple: a new baseball glove, a book on dinosaurs, and a baby doll for his little sister, May.

10. He wore the uniform of disaffected suburban youth: oversized clothing, slightly askew baseball hat, and multiple body piercings.

EXERCISE 52.5 Reviewing punctuation marks

SUGGESTED ANSWERS

2. Some parental efforts do help children; for instance, children whose parents read to them are more likely to enjoy books.

4. A new idea that is popular with many parents of young children is sign language.

6. By sixteen to eighteen months, most children are able to speak simple words and make themselves understood.

8. Garcia showed that parents could easily teach their children signs for words like *please, more, sleepy,* and *hungry.*

10. Not surprisingly, parents bought the book (and then the video), and now sign-language classes for small children are easy to find.

12. Correct

14. The researchers who developed the study said that the best reason for parents to sign with their children was to allow the children "to communicate what they need and see."

16. Others contend that the children's hand movements stand for concepts, so the movements are sign language.

18. In fact, children who can use sign language are often especially eager to learn how to speak.

20. Any activity that gets parents to spend more time communicating with their children probably has its benefits.

EXERCISE 53.1 Capitalizing

2. The Battle of Lexington and Concord was fought in April 1775.

4. Accepting an award for his score for the film *The High and the Mighty*, Dmitri Tiomkin thanked Beethoven, Brahms, Wagner, and Strauss.

6. We drove east over the Hudson River on the Tappan Zee Bridge.

8. "Bloody Sunday" was a massacre of Catholic protesters in Derry, Northern Ireland, on January 30, 1972.

10. The town in the American South where I was raised had a statue of a Civil War soldier in the center of Main Street.

EXERCISE 54.1 Using abbreviations

2. The power tools, ordinarily used for sanding wood, are placed on a thirty-foot track and plugged in; the sander to reach the end first wins.

4. There are three divisions of belt sander races: the stock division, which races sanders right out of the box; the modified division, which allows any motor the owner wants to add; and the decorative division, which provides a creative outlet for sander owners.

6. The fastest sanders run on very coarse sandpaper—a number sixteen grit is an excellent choice if it's available.

8. The S-B Power Tool Co. in Chicago, maker of Bosch sanders, allows participants to race its tools, but the company does not underwrite races.

10. No one knows what percentage of the nation's power tools have been used for this kind of entertainment.

EXERCISE 54.2 Spelling out numbers and using figures

SUGGESTED ANSWERS

2. You could travel around the city for only sixty-five cents. (*Or* Correct)

4. Correct

6. Correct (*Or* 25 cents)

8. Three hundred seven miles long and eighty-two miles wide, the island offered little of interest.

10. The department received 1,633 calls and 43 letters.

EXERCISE 55.1 Using italics

2. Regional writers produced some American classics, such as Mark Twain's *Huckleberry Finn* and James Fenimore Cooper's *Last of the Mohicans*.

4. Some of the most prolific regional writers were women like Kate Chopin, who wrote her first collection of short stories, *Bayou Folk*, to help support her family.

6. Chopin also departed from regional works to explore women's experiences of marriage, as in her short piece "The Story of an Hour."

8. She later turned these into a novel, *Deephaven*, which she hoped would "teach the world that country people were not . . . ignorant."

10. Many regional stories—Stephen Crane's "The Bride Comes to Yellow Sky" is a prime example—show the writer's concern that an isolated culture is in danger of disappearing.

EXERCISE 56.1 Using hyphens in compounds and with prefixes

2. my ex-mother-in-law
4. devil-may-care attitude
6. Correct
8. pro-NAFTA crowd
10. Correct

EXERCISE 56.2 Using hyphens appropriately

2. The House Un-American Activities Committee was formed in 1937.
4. Remember to drop off your medical forms.
6. Please remind Jane to pick up the clothes from the dry cleaners.

8. I have a nine-year-old daughter, and the younger one is nearly five years old.

10. The sign-up sheet is outside the gymnasium.

GLOSSARY OF USAGE

EXERCISE GU-1 Selecting the appropriate word

2. farther
4. fewer; than
6. discreet
8. lend
10. bad
12. may
14. continuous
16. with
18. flaunts
20. whether or not

EXERCISE GU-2 Editing inappropriate words

2. Correct
4. Johanna *hung* the sheets on the line because the fresh air made them smell good, but the neighbors complained.
6. The supervisor and the trainee speak to each other *every day*.
8. Correct
10. A small *percentage* of the graduates weren't qualified for the entry-level positions.
12. Swiss cheese is *different from* Jarlsberg.
14. Correct
16. She *immigrated* to New York in the 1920s.
18. My visiting relatives made *themselves* look like tourists by wearing white sneakers and by staring at all the tall buildings.
20. *It's hoped* that it won't rain during the company outing.

    OR

    We *hope* that it won't rain during the company outing.